For Barbara O'Brien,

True to my memory!

With love,

Mona

The Salt Cedars

Stories for My Daughter

By

Mona D. Sizer

iUniverse, Inc.
New York   Bloomington

The Salt Cedars
Stories for my Daughter

iUniverse books may be ordered through booksellers or by contacting:

iUniverse
1663 Liberty Drive
Bloomington, IN 47403
www.iuniverse.com
1-800-Authors (1-800-288-4677)

ISBN: 978-0-595-53416-6 (pbk)
ISBN: 978-0-595-63474-3 (ebk)

Printed in the United States of America

iUniverse rev. date: 12/29/2008

Instead of a Forward

Even before the birth of the new century, I realized that my youth was history. Even worse, it was soon to be lost history. My daughter would never know her personal heritage any more than I knew the lost youth of my great, great grandmother. I would never know what circumstances molded her into a woman of such power that she could summon up the skill and fortitude to save a soldier's life after the battle of Shiloh.

Still, I feel the impulse to convey that heritage within me extending through five generations to my daughter. I want her to know it does not come by accident. It was "bred in the bone," an expression that has somehow slipped from the language when Americans left the farms and ranches to depend on and value motors rather than fine horses. I want my daughter to feel the heritage of power that very well may be in her bones and spirit.

To that end, I acknowledge Rachel Andrea Sizer as the force that woke me at five o'clock every morning for weeks to stir my memories. Some were so sweet I smiled as I wrote. Some were so painful they made me weep. But for you, Daughter, they would have remained inside me.

My thanks to my many readers who have written or on occasion told me face to face how much they have enjoyed this book. Because of your encouragement, I have been most pleased to produce yet a third edition.

Thanks to James Sizer, my husband and Rachel's father, who helped and encouraged in the preparation of this manuscript.

Most of all, my eternal gratitude to my grandmother Vora Lee Stanfield Bevens, who told me the stories many time over as she showed me faded photographs and darkened tintypes some as old as the Civil War itself, until the people and their deeds were etched on my memory.

If I have misspoken, the fault is with my memory not my intent, for any memoir is about loss—the fault of time and distance, the loss of the beloved subjects as well as the most-beloved teller of the tales.

Mona D. Sizer
The Lower Rio Grande Valley of Texas

To Comfort Annis Lucinda Mahalah Woody Stanfield
To Fair-Eleanor Christine Craine Stanfield
To Vora Lee Stanfield Bevens
To Hona Helene Bevens Young

These women were your forebears.
I pass their stories on to you, Rachel Andrea.
I leave you a portion of my own story as well.
Make us your own.
Your spirit is the spirit of us all.

I
THE TREES

On the flat plain formed by the delta of the Rio Grande, the southern-most tip of Texas, we had a farm, a quarter section of good black bottomland with an artesian well that gushed forth fresh cold water with just the faintest trace of salt. My grandfather bought it in 1929 just before the depression paralyzed the United States.

He might have abandoned the acreage in 1930, cut his losses, and let it go for taxes as so many businessmen were doing in those bleak days. Fortunately, he couldn't. He had searched everywhere for that particular land. His need for it was grave—literally a matter of life and death.

During the 1930s he built three small "camp" houses on a country lane and erected a windmill and a water tower. He began to sell off his consider-able holdings in Booneville, Arkansas. For several years he brought my grand-mother down to "camp" to see how she liked it and how she fared in this strange new land. In 1935 he was making preparations for the move. He hired a master carpenter and contractor and set him to work drawing plans for big country manor house with every modern convenience.

Then he died—unexpectedly. Ironically.

My grandmother moved anyway. Although she must have spent many sleepless nights worrying and wondering, she left her house in Arkansas. She left the town where she was born with all her kin and friends around her. With no one but her younger daughter she moved into one of the "camp" houses. A short time later my mother and I moved too. In 1937 we were four females living in one small house at the end of a country lane.

The drive to the tiny town of Raymondville was seven miles beyond that lane on a farm-to-market road. For all intents and purposes we were iso-lated.

In front and to the east side of our farmhouse stood that rarest of the rare in that part of the world—a stand of tall trees. The prevailing wind from the

Gulf of Mexico, only twenty miles away, kept most trees twisted and stunted. But not these.

Because of the lowness of our land and the way the cedars huddled together to support each other, they had grown into a substantial windbreak that shielded our little house and the yard where I played.

Not only were the trees tall. They were without thorns.

Almost every native tree in South Texas has thorns. Especially vicious are coachwhip mesquite, bristling ebony, and killer huisache whose thorns are inch-long stilettos among slender frondlike leaves. A child can't climb these trees or push their branches aside, or even hide behind the trunks without suffering scratches and punctures.

But salt cedars are benign silken dreams of trees. Unlike northern cedars, their dark, dusty-green needles are soft fringes two to three inches long yet hardly bigger around than a piece of silk crochet thread. Their trunks are smooth and brown. Within days after the rain falls long and hard or the hurricane blows, sprays of tiny pinky-white flowers bloom on the ends of every frond.

Such trees were made to be the bowers of princesses, the hiding places of enchanted maidens in fairy tales, the trunks for lovers to carve initials, and—more to the point—ideal climbing gyms for a wild girl child.

Two of the trees had swings and another had a rope with knots and a loop on the end. Thinking back, I wonder how that makeshift gymnasium got there.

Did my grandmother—my Mammaw—climb the trees herself to attach the ropes? Did she—born in September of 1886—come down the front porch in the early morning dew to climb into the cedar boughs and tie those knots?

Did she, who never wore a pair of men's trousers or—shocking idea—a pair of shorts, shed her shoes and silk stockings, hike her skirt above her knees, reach up for handholds, place her bare feet in the tight crotches, and climb nine feet above the ground to attach cotton clothesline ropes for her granddaughter's pleasure?

Her task accomplished, did she scramble down, embarrassed, at haste to smooth her skirts decorously below her knees, roll up her hose, secure them tight around her thighs with binding garters, and slide her feet into her sensible black lace-up shoes?

Or did she pause astride the limb, lean back against the firm and solid trunk, let brightening sunlight bathe her face and gild her bare legs? Did she close her eyes and hear the Gulf breeze soughing through the cedars—the sound of the sea on land? Did she turn her cheek to let the silken needles caress her face?

Did she pray? A paean to the beauty of the God she loved. Did she dream? Of the one love lost forever who brought her to this place so far from everything she'd ever known?

Of course, as a child I never knew. She poured my milk, dished up my oatmeal, made the beds, sent me out to play. I'd race madly to the salt cedars, wrestle myself into the swings, kick my heels to the skies, and trail my head toward the ground. Laughing. Shouting. Pure delight.

Looking back, I wonder. The willingness to dare that's marked my life came from somewhere. Was it from the bold, ambitious man driven by love and desperation who bought and cleared the land and died? Or am I stronger akin to the loving, daring woman who followed him and stayed to hold it fast?

ππππ

If my grandmother found pleasure in the salt cedars, hers was nothing compared to my own. Those trees set me free of the earth. They gave me the sweeping, rushing motion that filled my imagination. They stoked my courage. They dared me to fly.

As a child of four, I'd gather the soft cotton clothesline rope in my hands, perch on a slanting limb some five feet about the ground, take a good high hold and swing—

Down and out in a great sweeping arc—

I'd grip the rope with my arms and hands. I'd stretch my bare feet and legs straight out before me. My body created a right angle in the air. My hair blew back. My skirt rucked up against my belly and fluttered behind me like a battle flag.

Out I'd fly, mouth open, drinking the rush of clean air, yelling like a soprano Tarzan. My feet would slam into the next tree. I'd bend my knees to absorb the force and sink into the trunk until my thighs would almost touch my chest. Then with a shout I'd push back and swing away in another direction, a second swing for the effort of one.

Like as not, I'd set myself spinning in ever shorter arcs and narrowing circles till finally I'd let my legs down and drag my bare feet on the ground.

I never let go the rope. Instead, I'd drape the rope over my shoulder and scramble up the tree again. This time I'd stand on another branch and put my foot in the loop at the rope's end. I'd hold tight and step off.

A shocking, exhilarating jerk at the end and then I was a wildly swinging pendulum. I'd thrust one leg and one arm out at right angles. I was a windmill. I was a whirligig. I was wild. I was free.

I was a bird. I was a plane. I was Supergirl. I was in a sublime gymnasium roofed by the sky, lit by the sun, and furnished by the salt cedars. Their ever-falling needles carpeted its floor. The equipment was limber living wood, the best the gods provide. It had never known a buzzsaw or a lathe.

I was a heathen worshiping in a temple that all the little savages pass through sooner or later. I was one of the wildest, one of the most daring.

Why? If I'd fallen, I might have broken something important—an arm, a leg? Why wasn't I timid? Where did I find the courage?

Of course, I'd seen Tarzan. If Johnny Weismuller could move from tree to tree in the RKO Radio jungle, I could move from tree to tree in the salt cedars. It wasn't as easy for me as it was for him because his jungle had many, many limbs. And almost all of them were straight and wide and ran parallel to the ground.

I didn't question his good fortune. I supposed that was the way trees grew in jungles. Many years later I discovered that they were the way trees were constructed on the back-lots of movie studios in Hollywood.

However, I learned to make do. If I climbed high enough and stepped out far enough, the branch where I stood would bow and bend down to allow me to put my foot onto a branch on the next tree. I had to be quick and then climb quicker because the branch I stepped on would bow away under my weight. There was a breathless moment between each tree when I was in both trees, yet not in either. I didn't even have a vine to cling to as Tarzan did.

How I loved it! I did it over and over again.

One evening in late summer my mother came home and saw me. She shrieked so loudly that I thought she'd seen one of the tarantulas that were known to live in salt cedars. I dropped flat on the limb and hung my head over it. I looked all around the ground trying to find the cause of such alarm. I was just about to tell her that tarantulas were more afraid of her than she was of them when she flung the car door open and bolted across the yard.

I stared at her. I was in no danger. I was Tarzan. I lived in trees. I lived in salt cedars.

Mammaw came running to the front porch in time to see Mother standing underneath me, holding up her arms, ordering me to come down before I broke my neck.

"Hona, what's wrong? What's happened to her?"

Mother was still trying to get me to come down.

I was afraid to let go. She couldn't quite reach me and I wasn't too sure that she wouldn't drop me.

"Did you see her?" she cried. "Did you see her? Come down from there this instant, Mona Dean."

Mammaw shook her head as she came down the steps and walked to her daughter's side. She looked up at me—all legs and arms. All bone, skin, and muscle. She smiled at me. "She'll be all right," she said to Mother.

"But those salt cedars are brittle," Mother argued. "She's up in the very top. If she falls, she'll kill herself."

"She won't fall," Mammaw assured her. She led my mother away. "Believe me," I heard her say. "She won't fall."

Mammaw knew me. Our kinship was a special bond stronger than the bond forged with my mother. Perhaps it came about because she had the care of me from the time I turned three till I went off to college. But that was only part of the relationship. A certain understanding lay between us—a recognition on her part that I was wilder than her own daughters. Perhaps she saw something of herself in me.

I only know that she encouraged me to be more than a demure, decorous little girl playing with dolls and reading instructive and inspiring books. She never sought to tamp the wildness down, only to channel it in the right directions.

Many times in the late morning, she sat on the porch-steps and watched me in those salt cedars. Did she sit with her heart in her throat, or did she join me in her heart in the heady swings and wild leaps?

I believe she was with me every moment, a part of the excitement. To her mind the joy was worth the risk.

To this day I've never *ever* fallen out of a tree.

II
THE BEGINNINGS

I couldn't swing through the salt cedars all the time. I'd have to come in when darkness fell. Sometimes it rained and sometimes Mammaw would decide that the heat was too intense for me to be playing outside.

Sometimes we'd lie back together on the daybed out on the sleeping porch and Mammaw would show me the pictures in the family albums. This happy circumstance gave my grandmother a chance to rest, look at the pictures of the people she loved. My grandmother was an only child whose family ties were far away in Arkansas. Sometimes she must have felt very lonely out there on the farm while Mother worked. Her mission on those occasions was to remember them and to teach me to remember them while she told me about my heritage.

One picture she told me about was of her grandmother who was a young woman during the Civil War. Booneville wasn't really touched, even though Arkansas seceded from the Union. Unfortunately, Mammaw's grandmother and grandfather lived in Tennessee, scene of one of the bloodiest battles of the war.

Mammaw's grandfather Thomas Peyton Stanfield, had joined the Wayne County unit of the Tennessee Volunteers. As a consequence of his patriotism, he died less than forty miles from his farm and his little family. On April 6, 1862, he fell at the battle of Shiloh, where thousands of American men and boys fighting on both sides lost their lives.

I thought the story that he died for States Rights very heroic without ever once thinking of the tragic circumstances he left behind. The old album has no picture of him, nor do I have a record of his birth. Since his sons were both short in stature, I can imagine him, a slight, frightened young man firing and returning fire across the Sunken Road. Perhaps he survived that engagement only to be ordered into the teeth of the cannons the Union had lined up at Peach Orchard. Perhaps he was wounded and crawled to Bloody Pond where he drank but was too weak to pull himself out of the water. Perhaps he lost consciousness and drowned as so many did. Perhaps he attacked Pittsburgh Landing in the evening only to die beneath the barrage from the Union gunboats on the Tennessee River.

My grandmother's eyes would shine with tears when she told the story. The battle of Shiloh was one of the South's greatest defeats, but my grandmother's heart was so tender, she wept for all the boys who died that day.

And she wept for her own grandmother who was left a widow with five little children to take care of. Her oldest son James Wayne Stanfield, Mammaw's father, was just five years old when his father was killed. His brother Joseph Zachariah was a year younger. His three little sisters, Mary, Comfort, and Charity were babies. Mammaw made sure I knew all the names so I'd remember them.

With her fatherless little children Comfort Annis Lucinda Mahalah Stanfield, whose maiden name was Woody, stayed on the little farm through the summer. Crops had been planted, so they weren't starving. Surely, neighbors would have helped her—if they had had enough to share.

But how must she have felt? Was she notified that her husband was dead and buried in a mass grave? Or did she hope and hope until finally she could hope no more?

I have two pictures of her taken years later by her son James, the photographer, my great-grandfather. They show her as an old woman with iron gray hair pulled back neatly from her high forehead. The pictures are remarkable. Her strong hand with nails clipped short rests over the head of a walking stick. Her dress is obviously fine, perhaps black or navy blue silk with ribbon trim on the yoke and cuffs. A silver bar pin graces the neck and another silver brooch pierces the fabric farther down at the edge of the yoke. She is slim, her waist clasped by a leather belt. She could be an ordinary well-to-do woman of her time with no more behind her than an ordered life of comparative leisure.

But the eyes are the windows of her soul. Her gaze is direct and penetrating, without pride or weakness, full of self-possession. It seems to say, "I have won through. I am content to meet whatever life has left for me."

"This is my grandmother," Mammaw would tell me, not proudly, but with a kind of wonderment. "She was so little she could stand under my arm.

"A wounded Confederate soldier staggered up the dirt lane to the farm. His arm had been shattered by cannon-fire. Pieces of white bone showed in the horrible wound. It was badly infected. Grandmother did what had to be done.

"She cut off his arm with a hacksaw, all but a flap of skin. She cleaned the wound, cauterized the blood vessels, and stitched the flap over the wound with silk embroidery thread."

My eyes must have been wide as saucers by that time. How could anyone cut off another person's arm? How could anyone stand to have an arm cut off? I couldn't imagine sticking a needle in a person's arm, much less pulling it through and out again.

"And he lived. She nursed him and when he was strong enough, he thanked her and went back home where he lived to grow old.

"She did all that." Mammaw would tell me reverently. "And she was only twenty-two."

Twenty-two seemed very old when I was four, but now I understand that my grandmother was just as much in awe as I was. Where had that tiny woman found that kind of strength?

As Mammaw resumed the tale, I could hear the echoes of another in her voice. I know now she was repeating the tale her grandmother had told her.

"That fall when the corn was about to be harvested, a troop of Union soldiers camped on her place. They picketed their horses in the cornfield and ate from the family's larder. When they rode on, there was almost nothing left.

"My poppa and his brother went out where the picket line had been strung and gleaned the corn that had fallen from the horses' mouths. Grandmother parched it and ground it and they lived on it that winter."

I remember her shaking her head again as if she couldn't believe what she was about to tell me.

"After the war the State of Tennessee paid her a pension of twenty-eight dollars a month. That was all she had to raise her children on."

She told her story to me so often that I knew the words by heart. I heard Mammaw's voice in my ears relating the deeds of her grandmother. She didn't intend that I should ever forget them. And I never have. As I write for you, Rachel Andrea, I am repeating them word for word.

"She was only twenty-two years old."

From deep within her Comfort Annis Lucinda Mahalah found the strength to do what had to be done, to take care of her household, her family, and even a stranger who came in need of help. Was he a Yankee or a Rebel? Probably it didn't matter. He was a suffering human being. She was a woman of infinite grace and fortitude.

She died January 30, 1908, just two and a half weeks after her great grandchild, my mother, was born. She lived to see her. I can believe she stayed alive for that purpose because Mammaw lived almost by will alone to see you, Rachel Andrea, her first great grand-daughter. She died six weeks later to the day.

Only one thing more should be recorded. When you were a little girl, Rachel, we visited Shiloh Battlefield. At the memorial park and cemetery headquarters, *you*, not I, asked to see the final roster of names of men who perished there. In a silver-gray book among the Wayne County troops of the Tennessee Volunteers was the name of your great-great-great grandfather Thomas Peyton Stanfield.

More than a hundred years separated you, but the connection was made by the stories my grandmother told me. A valediction and a validation of families and of love.

ππ π

As we looked through the family albums, I saw so many, many photos of my great grandfather James Wayne Stanfield. Even though he'd died fourteen years before I was born, I almost felt as if I could remember him. Whenever we returned to Booneville, older people who remembered him would speak to me about Uncle Jim, a cheery, rotund man, who was such a good fellow. Everybody loved him.

I'm sure I would have loved him too, but I wondered a bit about him. Mammaw was packed and ready to go away to "normal school" to study to be a teacher when he talked her out of it. He begged his only daughter to forego the education she truly longed for. He wanted her to stay home because he loved her so much, he couldn't be without her.

He assured her that she didn't need a profession. He had enough money to take care of her for the rest of her life. What made his assurances so ironic was that he seldom worked in the general store and the Bank of Booneville, both businesses that he and his brother owned, businesses that had come to him from his mother. His wife, my great grandmother, ran them both and made them very profitable.

Her stewardship allowed him to play the cheery grasshopper married to the industrious practical ant. He followed his various pursuits while she cultivated the family fortune.

I inherited the violin he is reputed to have played very well. I'm sure I would have loved him too. Who wouldn't be happy playing and singing in the sunshine in the meadow? Unfortunately, I never learned to play the instrument. Not a single person in the Rio Grande Valley knew how to play the violin in 1938, much less give lessons on it.

Thank heaven we treasured it and kept it. I had it appraised before Rachel wanted to join the orchestra. The appraiser didn't know how to value it. He had never seen anything like it, but he reported that it had a beautiful tone, so my daughter learned to play on her great-great grandfather's violin.

Mammaw also passed on to us several notebooks containing his literary works—beautiful sentiments of the time—essays and *belles lettres* written in an exquisite copperplate hand and illustrated at intervals with line drawings in red and blue as well as black inks.

Mammaw would show me the two cigar boxes of old watches and the jewelry box containing her pieces of 18-carat gold jewelry. My great grandfather designed and crafted my grandmother's engagement ring in gold with a pearl and an emerald set in an exquisite setting at his store. He was a watchmaker as well as a jeweler. That is to say he repaired clocks and watches. He didn't actually make them. When he died, our family inherited timepieces of all sizes. The largest was a grandmother clock over four feet long made to hang on a wall, its pendulum swinging back and forth, its ticking echoing in the room. The smallest was a lady's lapel watch with a sterling silver case.

With all these talents and skills, he never worked hard at anything. He loved to spend time fishing and lolling away the sunny hours. Someone, probably Mammaw, took a photograph of him standing on the creek-bank in the bright sunlight. His clothes are rumpled, his shirt is without a collar, his hat is tipped back on his head. He is holding a huge bass. Its mouth is level with his belt. Its tail touches the ground.

My grandmother's expression was always loving when she showed us that picture.

"Poppa fell in the water that day," she'd tell me. "We were all on a picnic." "We" were the pupils in the Sunday school class he taught. "We heard this great big splash. Everybody cried, 'Oh, Mr. Stanfield's caught a big fish!' We all ran down to the bank and he'd fallen in headfirst. But he climbed out with a big smile on his face."

Mammaw and I would giggle together at the thought of my tubby little great-grandfather falling into a creek headfirst. He must have been such a good sport. From his daughter I heard nothing but loving and often humorous stories about her beloved father. How I wished I could have had a grandfather who would take me fishing.

He became interested in photography. Somewhere around 1889 or 1890, he took a tintype picture of the two of them when she looks to have been between three and four. He is seated, looking so young and handsome with his neatly trimmed moustache.

His left hand hangs at his side where he concealed the long cable he used to snap the picture. His right arm is curved around her. She stands on a stool beside his chair leaning trustingly against his side. Later he enlarged the picture and tinted it. It remains today a beautiful relic in a velvet-matted frame—a picture of love.

πππ

Mammaw had well over a hundred photographs her father made of her friends, her husband, her children, and her—so many of her. The odd thing is that after all the pictures he took of Mammaw and every cousin or girlfriend that ever walked down the street, he took almost none of his wife.

He married Fair-Eleanor Christine in 1885. He was twenty-eight, she was twenty-nine. She was the daughter of Jeremiah Vardeman Craine, a stern-faced patriarch, who had lived in the valley of the Petit Jean since Arkansas became a territory in 1819.

James Stanfield was a relative stranger to the small town. His mother had moved the family from Tennessee to Arkansas in 1880. To this day I wonder how the marriage of the well-to-do landowner's daughter and the newcomer came about.

Fair-Eleanor Christine Craine must have been a woman to stand against the tide. She certainly had a singular mind unburdened—in the way that very few women are—by the softer sensibilities.

She was tiny person, quite gaunt. I have another photograph taken of her in her youth. Even then she possessed the porcelain skin and fine features of a French doll. Part of her hair is rolled about the top of her head, like a crown. The rest hangs loose, long and wavy down over her shoulders like a veil. She is staring directly into the lens with a doll's impassivity.

But she was no doll. Legend has it that she was the driving force in the marriage. She kept the account books in a clear efficient hand. She ran the businesses while her artistic, gifted husband pursued his hobbies and arranged his pleasures. How very, very different they were!

Mammaw didn't have pictures to show me of Fair-Eleanor Christine standing on a creek-bank, nor sitting in a chair with an affectionate arm around her little daughter. She showed me the only picture that I know that her husband took of her. It shows a serious-faced woman in an elegant fitted suit.

Looking very much the woman of property, she sits for the camera, her expression a bit haughty, her eyes direct. She is beautiful in an icy way. The sheen of her suit indicates that it is very probably silk taffeta or faille. White ruffles stand up around her throat out of the fur collar both deep and wide. In her lap she holds what must have been the most elegant hat in Booneville,

Arkansas, a clipped beaver with a wide brim with feathers curling over it. She doesn't smile.

Undoubtedly she was too busy working at the bank and the store to pose for silly pictures or fish from the creek-bank—or smile.

One wonders. Did she try to focus her husband's life to fit her father's pattern? When the man she married resisted, did she focus her own and leave him to his own pursuits. Did she go to the bank or the general store each morning and leave him to play with his daughter? Did they maintain mutual love and respect for each other? What was their marriage really like?

There was no such thing as prevention of pregnancy by contraception, yet they only had one child born in September of 1886.

They were real people in a time when divorce was not possible. Their problems must have been ones people don't usually associate with great-great grandparents.

Surely extended family histories shed some kind of light on their true relationship or at least leads to speculation. Fair-Eleanor's older sister Mary Magdalene had eleven children. Her younger sister Laura Belle had four. Moreover, no one that I ever heard talked about Fair-Eleanor Christine except in superlatives odd for a woman. Not the kindest and dearest—but shrewdest and strongest. Neither my mother nor my Aunt Jane spoke of loving their grandmother—only of remembering her.

Once when my Aunt Jane was slashing at everyone in sight with her tongue like a well-honed straight razor, my mother quieted her with a telling accusation and a stare that left volumes unsaid.

"You sound just like Grandmother."

Aunt Jane's mouth snapped shut as if she never meant to open it again. Her jaw clenched. She glared at my mother. Then she dropped her gaze and stalked away.

My mother told me only that Fair-Eleanor died before I was born. "She never got to see you," she said.

She did not say, "She would have loved you."

How did she feel about her only child, her heir? How did she regard the obvious affection that her husband showered on their daughter?

Mammaw told me only one tale that sheds light on her relationship with her mother. Along with all the happy stories of Poppa and Sunday school and fishing trips, she told one story from her childhood that sounds straight out of a Charles Dickens novel.

Mammaw had been left at home to do chores while her mother ran down to the store to do the accounts. Her particular task was to iron her father's shirts. Mammaw was only eight or nine. In 1895 without electricity, flatirons had to be heated on a woodstove and lifted off with potholders.

At least two irons were in use at all times, one on the stove and one in use on the ironing board. As it cooled, the person doing the ironing exchanged it for the hot one, working swiftly, to keep the sprinkled, starched clothes from drying out and getting "cat faces."

"I cried and cried," Mammaw said. "I kept scorching them."

"What happened?" I touched her hand in real sympathy. I'd never had to do any ironing, but I could imagine how hard it was. "Was the iron too hot?"

"When Momma got home, she discovered that she'd used baking soda instead of starch," Mammaw explained.

"So it wasn't your fault." I sat back relieved. "You weren't to blame. She didn't get mad at you."

Mammaw's smile looked at little twisted.

Suddenly, I knew that her mother had been angry with her. I rubbed my arms to push the goosebumps back into the skin.

My Mammaw's cousins, particularly Aunt Frank, spoke almost reverently of "Auntie." When Laura Belle, Fair-Eleanor's sister died, she gave Aunt Frank to her sister to rear, in the time-honored way of small town relationships a hundred years ago. In those days there were no orphans. Everyone provided everyone else's social security.

But after Mammaw died, Aunt Frank wept as if her heart would break. She admitted to me that while she revered "Auntie," she loved my grandmother. Mammaw was the one who really reared her. She was the one who loved her and made up for the loss of her mother.

Fair-Eleanor remains an enigma. Did she choose to do as she did? Or was she driven into the bank and store by her fun-loving husband? Did her husband allow her the running of his life and the making of his fortune because he was used to his mother's doing so? Why did she work so hard? Did she labor to keep body and soul together or to buy the finer things symbolized by the silk taffeta suit and the beaver hat with the gleaming black feathers? Did she hate what she did? Did she love it?

Whatever she was, she left behind her own legend and a very different legacy from her husband's. She put steel in all our spines.

We'd put the old albums aside and open the newer ones. They were more interesting anyway. Pictures of my mother, glamorous studio portraits from Chicago and Atlanta, pictures of Aunt Jane in her fun-loving college days, cut all too short by her father's death. Pictures of me. My grandmother must have looked at her two daughters and her granddaughter with fond amazement.

My mother Hona Helene was a cool brunette autumn night with clouds half-obscuring the moon and stars, vagrant breezes carrying the scents of hyacinth and wood smoke.

My aunt Fair-Eleanor Jane was a blazing red-haired sun in a summer sky at noon with dust devils constantly swirling the mirages. In her character the sweetness of roses mingled with the bitterness of careless weed.

I was like neither of them—wild, tantrum-prone, risk-taking, reared alone, the center of my own universe. I thought the world revolved around me.

Mammaw did her best to make ladies of us all. We took her education; we loved her unreservedly. She was the standard for our lives—a standard which she adapted to suit her own personality. It reflected facts from both her mother and her grandmother who'd gone before.

Because of her example, we are the women that we are—determined to have what we believe we are entitled to have. It hasn't been handed to us on a silver platter. Not one platter has any of us caught more than a fleeting glimpse of. So we've had to get it on our own.

But we will not allow anyone or anything to shove us aside. We will not be defeated.

$$\pi\pi\pi$$

How my grandmother maintained her courage and wrestled with death itself is a story that I cherish more than all the other memories. How close her grandmother must have been to her in spirit and how strength flowed from one woman to the other borders on the supernatural.

The valley of the Petit Jean admitted newcomers slowly. Far from the rivers of commerce—the mighty Arkansas, the Red, and the Ouachita—it was a country of cousins where a man or a woman was related to everyone she met either on her mother's or her father's side. The town was small enough that everyone helped everyone else. It was also a country where the spirits of the dead walked among the living, unseen perhaps but offering comfort in time of need. Every time Mammaw took me back to the homeplace, we visited the cemetery. I always felt comfortable there as if I were being welcomed.

We'd walk up the hill to a grove of cedar trees at least a hundred years old. There Pawpaw's father and mother were buried with all his little brothers and sisters who had died young of many childhood diseases that modern babies get vaccinated against as a matter of course. We'd look at the names and dates on the tiny tombstones and I'd want to cry. Some of them had only lived a few months before they went to Heaven.

They say Heaven is a beautiful place. So at least part of it must be an Arkansas cemetery with cedar trees now a couple of centuries old. I didn't doubt their spirits had dwelt there.

The spirits were there in earlier times because they were needed. They were part of the plan of things. Mammaw knew because she'd encountered one that she never doubted and never forgot.

She told me the story at least once in the cemetery while I shuddered, and cold chills ran up and down my arms. Then she told me again and again because I asked her to. I wanted to be sure to remember her experience exactly as it happened.

Pawpaw was very ill. He had pneumonia in the days before penicillin and oxygen tents. Mammaw had his bed set up in the kitchen where the huge wood-burning stove made the room the warmest in the house. As with all houses built at the dawn of the twentieth century, the kitchen was an added-on room at the back of the house because of the heat it generated in the summer and the danger of fire.

Mammaw's cousin Blanche had come to stay, but she had gone to sleep in the upstairs bedroom facing out onto the front street.

My grandfather was six-foot-four and weighed over two hundred pounds. My grandmother was five-foot-six and weighed probably a hundred ten. Hour after hour, she'd sat beside his bed while he slept. His breathing was ragged, rattling in his chest. She kept putting cold cloths on his head and neck to keep his fever down. From time to time she rolled out hot bricks from the oven to wrap in towels and put near his feet that had poor circulation because of his diabetes.

At last, exhausted, she put her head down on the bed by his hand.

Gradually, like a dawning realization, she felt something, heard something, *knew* something. She sat up startled.

A man stood in the doorway of the dining room. Not really in the doorway, but beyond the doorway with the darkness all round him. His dark suit blended with it. Above his white shirt and high white collar, his features were indistinct in the shadows, but his eyes pierced the darkness.

She stared at him, stared into his eyes. She could feel the skin prickling on her arms and the hair rising on the back of her neck, but she wasn't afraid. She waited.

He nodded gently. Then he stepped backward into the darkness that closed round him like a cloak.

When she looked down, Pawpaw's eyes were open. "What's wrong," he whispered.

She put her hands on his face and body. As she clutched him, she shuddered so hard her teeth clicked together. He was alive. Please, God! She was so afraid that he going to die—that the man had come for him.

"Nothing," she said. "I just dozed off and had a dream. Go back to sleep."

Not for one moment did she think a living man had somehow come into the house. But something, someone had. She knew she hadn't had a dream. When Pawpaw's eyes closed, she left his side. She had to steel herself at the door. Her skin was hot and cold by turns. She was holding herself so tightly against the rising panic that she could barely walk. But she took a deep breath and rushed into the darkness.

Through the empty dining room into the hall, she fled to climb the steep staircase. The house was dark. Only her footsteps sounded on the carpeted risers. At the top of the stair, a solid oak door was kept closed to prevent heat from rising and leaving the downstairs cold. Opening it, she hurried down the hall and into the room where Blanche was sleeping.

Her cousin awakened with a start. "What's wrong, Vora?"

"Nothing," my grandmother said. "Get dressed and come down."

Once they were in the kitchen, she stirred up the fire and began to make her cousin some cocoa.

Pawpaw stopped breathing!

Seventy years ago life-saving techniques consisted of a sort of primitive artificial respiration. But Pawpaw was twice Mammaw's size. His arms, long and heavily muscled, flopped when she tried to raise them. Blanche's help was absolutely necessary to push on his chest while my grandmother pumped his arms to keep his lungs expanding and contracting. They worked on him almost half an hour before he caught his breath and began breathing on his own again.

As Mammaw lifted Pawpaw's arms over his head and lowered them, she kept glancing at the door to the dining room, but no one was there. She knew if she hadn't awakened Blanche, she would have lost Pawpaw. Blanche would never have heard her screams from her bed in the front of the house, and Mammaw wouldn't have had the strength to do both movements at once.

Later after she'd made him comfortable and Blanche was drinking a cup of hot cocoa, Mammaw took a lamp through every room on the first floor of the house. Every room was empty. Nothing had been disturbed. No window was open even a crack. No door stood ajar. No one was there who shouldn't be.

Still, she never thought she'd dreamed her visitor. She *knew* she'd been warned.

The next night about midnight she was on watch again. Pawpaw was breathing more easily. His cough had lessened. He'd eaten something during the day and sat up for an hour. Although his fever still hadn't broken, Cousin Blanche had gone to bed because he seemed so much improved.

Mammaw heard a knock on the door. So late at night, she was almost afraid to answer it, but this was a country town. No one who wasn't a friend or relative would be there.

Sure enough, John Diehl, one of Pawpaw's cousins several times removed, stood there. He had a strange, drawn look on his face.

"Something told me to come," he told Mammaw. He glanced around warily. "Is Noah all right? Something told me I'd better come over."

Mammaw didn't ask what. She didn't want him to think she was crazy. She didn't dare to tell him what had told her to get Blanche out of bed the night before.

She poured her guest a cup of coffee. Just as John took his first sip, Pawpaw stopped breathing again. This time with John's strength and help, Mammaw was able to revive him quickly.

All night long John stayed with them, helping her nurse his cousin. At dawn the fever broke. He helped her change the damp sheets and Pawpaw's soaked nightshirt.

Shortly after dawn Cousin Blanche woke. Pawpaw was sleeping peacefully. His lungs had begun to clear.

For Mammaw the truth of what happened to her and to John Diehl was clear and she told it fearlessly—testified to her granddaughter about her experience.

She cherished her belief that every human being had a purpose in life. That life went on so long as that purpose was not achieved. My grandfather was saved because he had more to do. He had more to accomplish for his family. He lived to play a pivotal part in her future and the future of us all.

III
THE VALLEY

Why did we come to the Rio Grande Valley?

Why did my grandfather search out this particular piece of land and bring us eight hundred miles from the place where we were all born?

The answer lies in geography.

At one time nearly all of Texas was under the Gulf of Mexico. The majestic Cap Rock rising in a fortress line across the western horizon in the Panhandle of Texas was the beachhead of this deeper, larger ancient sea. When it receded, it left some of the richest and lowest land in America.

Low land was what my grandfather sought. Low land that could be farmed in the way that he understood. Low land that would save his wife's life.

Mammaw couldn't walk up three flights of stairs or ride an elevator to the third floor in a tall building without literally losing her breath. The first time I remember seeing this happen, I was terrified.

She gave a great gasp and then another. Her nose pinched together with the force of her effort to pull in enough air to keep from losing consciousness. Her face turned red and then, as it lost the battle, turned paler and paler. Her lips lost color. Her hands grew cold. As her blood carried less oxygen, her feet and ankles began to turn blue. She dared not speak for fear of losing her breath.

Over the years the strange attacks varied neither in their instances nor in their duration. Always if she went up too high too fast or stayed too long, she would lose her breath.

If she took the elevator slow and easy, that is getting off on the second floor and sitting quietly for a quarter of an hour, she could then go to the third. Once we moved to the Valley, she could acclimate herself gradually to the rising land on our way eight-hundred mile drives for a visit to Booneville. Of course, we had to pick our routes. We couldn't go by way of Texarkana and turn north because of the mountains at Mena, Arkansas. We had to go north through McAlester, Oklahoma, and turn east.

Even then Mammaw's best efforts—quiet meditation while she drank hot coffee with plenty of sugar—sometimes weren't successful. She would have a frightening attack.

It was all the more frightening because no one seemed to be able to help her. She had to overcome it herself. When I grew a little older, I asked Mammaw how it felt not to be able to breathe in enough air. She shook her head. She would never describe the experience to me.

My mother told me that the first attack happened when Mammaw and Pawpaw were driving along on their way to Methodist Church Conference in Eureka Springs. As they climbed higher among some of the most beautiful mountains of the Ozarks, she lost her breath with a harsh gasp. He looked at her, but she had clapped her hand over her mouth and was looking straight ahead. He thought she was mad at him because she wouldn't speak to him.

She wasn't angry. She was smothering. She was terrified. All through the conference, she felt woozy and ill. She kept losing her breath and having to sit down. She stayed in the hotel room during most of the meetings and services. She was afraid to go to sleep. As the hours passed, her breathlessness, her feelings of smothering increased. She began to be afraid she would die before she got down out of the mountains.

Later, she went to doctors in Fort Smith about her condition, but they could tell her nothing. They smiled gently and shook their heads. One even went so far as to insult her by suggesting that she have a hysterectomy to get rid of her "female hysteria." In those days any woman's problem that a male doctor couldn't immediately diagnose was put down to hysteria.

Doctors did very little testing and diagnosing seventy-five years ago. Symptoms were treated with quinine and the much newer aspirin. A person could be purged to "clean them out." Wounds could be made antiseptic with alcohol or carbolic acid or painted with iodine. Broken bones could be set. Cuts could be stitched and closed although not without danger of infection around the thread as it rotted in the holes.

But Mammaw had none of these problems. Time after time, Pawpaw would try to talk to medical men begging them for some sort of explanation. They would look at him blankly. Then they would inquire, "The lady lost her breath?"

"Yes."

"Did she die?"

"No, but—"

"Well, then—" They would simply spread their hands. "Female hysteria. The female mind is incapable of handling many of the more difficult situations. It simply swoons. She'll recover consciousness and be none the worse. It's their delicate natures."

They gave her nothing at all with which to fight her battle. She had no portable oxygen tank to wheel around with her. They had no MRI to find out what was going on somewhere inside her body. Such things simply didn't exist.

She had to fight her battle all alone. It was the battle to stay awake, for she was sure that if she lost consciousness, she wouldn't be able to pull in enough air to breathe. Thank heaven, she was a fighter! How terrible to have to fight so hard simply to breathe!

The situation was getting worse when Pawpaw heard of the Valley: New land. Newly opened for settlement. Fertile farmland. Delta land. Bottomland. And best of all—only a hundred feet above sea level.

As quickly as he possibly could he bought two acreages—one improved, one unimproved. He contracted with Harley Warren, a carpenter, who moved his wife Lillian and his four children, two sons and two daughters to the Valley to build three small houses on the improved quarter section. Eventually, Harley was supposed to have built a new mansion, a new homeplace.

Of course, Pawpaw had to be sure that the Valley was right for Mammaw. At first they vacationed—camped, as she called it. Then they spent summers in Arkansas and winters in Texas.

Gradually, she realized she didn't feel quite as strong in Arkansas.

In December of 1935, he went to the Valley to make the preparations for their move. Though he appeared healthy, his body was undermined by grave illnesses—diabetes and high blood pressure. His diabetes in particular plagued him constantly. Making the eight hundred mile drive alone taxed his strength. He arrived ill. His illness turned into pneumonia.

Mammaw received the news by telegram that he was in the hospital in Raymondville, the closest town to the farm. She and her younger daughter my Aunt Jane drove without stopping from Booneville in the snow and ice of December. She reached his side on Christmas Eve. He died the next morning.

His death devastated her. Unprepared and alone, she had to make the choice to leave everything she had ever known—home, family, and friends— to go to live among strangers.

In the midst of overwhelming grief, she had to make a decision. She was forty-nine, a survivor of cancer and the strange disease the doctor's called "female hysteria." Her older daughter was married and living with her husband and their baby daughter in Heavener, Oklahoma. Mammaw and her younger daughter who was twenty would be facing a new frontier alone.

With remarkable courage, she chose the path he'd opened for her. She didn't go back to Booneville. She belonged to the Valley where she could breathe free.

πππ

I've told why my grandmother came to the Valley, but not why my mother and I came. We didn't move there immediately in 1936 because my mother had married a "handsome devil" of a man. And she wanted so much to believe that he hadn't "done her so wrong."

When my mother and father were first married long before I was born into their lives, he suggested a trip from Greenwood, Arkansas, to Poteau, Oklahoma, and on to Heavener, where his father and mother lived. Of course, Mother went along. She was always up for fun in those days. They were young and free to take off on "larks" in the middle of the night.

On a gravel road in the light of a three-quarter moon, they'd run over a piece of glass or picked up a nail or some other piece of debris. The result was a flat tire.

In those days a flat tire meant actually changing a tire—not changing a wheel as is done today. The old '29 Ford, had to be jacked up, the wheel taken off and laid on the ground. Then the inner tube had to be pulled out of the tire and replaced with a spare (if such a thing were available). The nail or glass had to be removed from the tire, and on and on. A patch kit and a tire pump were involved. It was hard, greasy work that might have to be repeated if the trip were long enough. Sometimes a thirty mile trip might be marked with an amazing report—only one flat.

Mother found the flashlight while my father opened the trunk and pulled out the equipment. He closed the trunk hastily as the lights of another car appeared in the distance. He placed the jack under the bumper and jacked the car off the ground. He just about had the lug nuts loose from the wheel when the car pulled up behind them.

My father threw a glance over his shoulder and almost fell over. He looked up at my mother.

"My God, Hona," he whispered. "We're driving a tanker."

Mother felt a hot burst of anger, then an icy chill of fear. How could he have been so foolish? How could he have put their future and their reputations, not to speak of their lives, in jeopardy?

She was so mad she wanted to turn on her heel, climb in the car and drive off, leaving him kneeling there. If not for the fact that the rear wheel was on the ground she probably would have.

The Arkansas State Trooper climbed out of his car, noted the license number and strolled into the lights. "Out pretty late, ain't cha?"

Mother was shaking. A "tanker" was any car loaded with jugs or sometimes hidden tanks containing illegal alcohol. She had visions of both her and my father being arrested on federal charges instituted by the Eighteenth Amendment to the Constitution, the Prohibition Amendment. If they got caught transporting illegal moonshine whiskey, they could both go to jail even though she hadn't known what the car was carrying. For a fleeting moment she had to struggle not to brain him with the flashlight. Worst of all, in her estimation was that the law would take the car, and they were driving *her* car. Her father had bought it for her when she'd graduated from college.

"*It's your turn to think fast, bub,*" she thought.

My father slowly straightened.

The trooper tucked his thumbs into his belt. His voice was gruff, laced with suspicion. He was pretty sure he'd caught a pair of moonshiners. "What y'all doin' out so late?"

Mother knew the lawman was standing barely a yard away from the locked trunk. If he ordered them to open it, he would catch them both. She dropped the flashlight and began to giggle. Clasping her hands behind her, she pulled off her wedding ring and slipped it into her pocket. She'd been trained for the stage and had been teaching speech and expression in Heavener when my father had married her. She rolled her eyes and brushed a lock of naturally-curly brown hair from her forehead.

"Please, sir," she said. "We're eloping." Then she burst into another fit of nervous giggles.

My father put his arm around her waist and hugged her against his side. He shuffled his feet and kicked at the gravel in the roadbed.

The trooper grunted. He stooped and picked up the flashlight and swept it up and down the two of them. Mother hid her face in my father's shoulder. My father flashed his best he-man smile.

Then the trooper grinned. "Well, now, looks like y'all need help with that tire?"

My father's nerves were strung tight by that time. He and his older brother Orr had a more-than-speaking acquaintance with some of the most notorious of the southwest's bootleggers as well as more dangerous outlaws including Pretty Boy Floyd and Bonnie Parker and Clyde Barrow. Mother could feel my father's pulse beating and his muscles jumping under his shirt.

He hugged her again and kissed her. She giggled some more and flashed the trooper her biggest smile.

Then my father patted her lovingly and dropped down on one knee. "If you'd hold the light," he said, "I'll have the tube in here in a jiffy. Then I'd appreciate it if you'd help me pump her up."

So the state trooper helped the amateur bootlegger and his "kewpie doll" change their flat just a few inches from a trunk-load of gallon jars of one hundred proof Ouachita moonshine.

Mother giggled and thanked him. My father shook his hand. He waved them on their way.

When I heard the story from my Aunt Jane, mother's sister, I didn't believe her. My quiet reserved mother would never, never break the law. My mother would never lie, never steal, never be part—even accidentally—of anything illegal.

Of course, my father would. He was what local Arkansas gossip referred to as "a real stampeder." My memories of him were vivid and mostly unpleasant.

As I grew and got myself involved in minor scrapes, I developed more tolerance for my mother. Recently, I've though about how quick she was, how resourceful, how with her acting she averted what would have been a disaster precipitated by her foolish husband.

In the twenty-first century my parents' sins seem minor, totally understandable, and even acceptable. Compared with the crazy things young people do today, my mother seems a model of proper behavior. All women with any spirit do crazy things. And certainly somewhere in every woman's past, she is entitled to at least a speaking acquaintance with a "handsome devil." My mother was just unlucky enough to marry one.

ππππ

Mother had a professional photograph of my father that she put out for my benefit. He had a pleasant-enough face, I suppose. She also had a small album of Kodak snapshots I could look through. They might as well have been pictures of a stranger.

What I couldn't understand was why everyone said I looked just like him. I couldn't see the resemblance at all. Of course, I had blue eyes, but so did Aunt Jane. Weren't my blue eyes like hers? I was tall for my age and lanky, but she was slender and taller than my mother. As for my mother. She looked like a mother. It's not at all strange that I still think that all mothers should look like her. I loved her then uncritically…and today, I love her memory even more because I realize what she did for me.

Of course, my grandmother must have read my character from the very beginning. I was a wild child. The frenetic behavior, the temper tantrums, the stomping and screaming when I couldn't have my way, everything she attributed to my being Fred Young's daughter. She set her sights on rearing someone who was at least civilized. I would not be a "little devil."

In other words, I would not be spoiled in the real sense of the word from those days and times. Homilies like "Pretty is as pretty does," and "Speak when you're spoken to," were ever on her lips. She firmly believed that if she didn't require me to learn self-discipline, I would be ruined for life.

She had no use for Fred Young, particularly after she heard about the episode with the trooper. In her opinion serious, responsible people did not break the law. Her son-in-law had chosen to do it because he wanted to have an adventure and make a little money while he did so. Prohibition was against the law for a good reason. It was not an adventure. My grandmother believed he had been badly spoiled. In other words, he had been ruined.

How right she was!

He was the younger of two sons, the tall blue-eyed one whose family catered to him. He had rheumatic fever as a child and the disease damaged his heart. Once in a while, he would pass out. He would fall from his chair at the dinner table or pitch over at his desk in school. These collapses caused a great and undoubtedly satisfying commotion. The perfect disturbance to draw maximum attention to himself. His mother, of course, ran to fetch pillows. His brother was told to fetch a pillow and straighten his limbs. Teachers at school were alerted and instructed to do the same.

When he joined the Bevens family, he told Mammaw what might occur. He said she was not to worry. He'd recover if he were left alone. Mammaw smiled gently with the barest trace of steel.

The first time he pitched out of the chair at the supper table, my mother started to go to his aid. Mammaw stopped her immediately. Quietly but firmly, she told everyone to stay seated and go on eating. She introduced a new topic of conversation. In an amazingly short time, he recovered consciousness and climbed back into his chair. Mammaw smiled brightly and passed the ham.

He never passed out at her table again.

Since Pawpaw owned the whole block and, with his brother Bas, the Bank of Booneville, my mother and father were able to secure a bank loan to build a new home next door to Mammaw and Pawpaw. No collateral was necessary. At the same time my parents went into business. My father signed a contract with Sinclair Oil Company to open a service station attached to a small café where the Continental Trailways bus would stop for lunch.

Father would run the station; Mother would cook and serve the lunches. They were secure. Their future looked bright. All they had to do was work hard and go to church regularly. All should have been bliss.

But my father's wild, spoiled streak began to dominate his life. His temper was legendary as well as his foul language when he threw a fit. Time and again, Mother warned him about cursing in front of me.

On most days she brought me with her while she prepared the lunches and served the passengers in the little café on Booneville's main street. Consequently, I was frequently in the presence of my father.

One particularly windy day I came running to her with news. "Mother! Mother! The god damn sign's blowing down the street!"

Indeed the circular metal Sinclair sign had broken loose, crashed to the ground, and was rolling and bouncing down the main street.

Several diners eating at the counter and at the small tables reacted differently. Some faces registered frozen disapproval; others, amused tolerance. Mother heaved a sigh. Then she smiled. "Go tell your father, sweetheart."

As she watched from the window, I ran up to him and repeated my news in front of several customers at our service station. His eyes widened. He pulled me against his leg as he grinned and apologized to them. From that time on he toned down his vocabulary.

πππ

I don't remember this incident. My mother told me about it in an effort to offer a suitable explanation when I asked why we weren't living with him any more.

I, however, had my own opinion.

I remember him clearly in my mind's eye, his image blazoned forever when I was only two years old. My memory is two pictures of violent acts that he perpetrated. The only true picture of have of my father's face is that of a monster.

As I've said, Mother's photographs show a pleasant-faced man with dark straight hair, even features, a firm chin, a cool smile, and light eyes that show almost no color in the black and white pictures. They are the blue he passed on to me and then to his granddaughter Rachel.

He had a flare for the dramatic. One picture shows him sitting casually on a big boulder beside a creek. He has one foot on the ground, the other propped jauntily on a smaller boulder.

He's wearing what appear to be knee-high lace-up boots and jodhpurs. His shirt is white and his high-crowned hat is cream-colored. I've never seen an outfit like it outside of a Western movie wherein the hero was building Boulder Dam. Certainly, no one else dressed like that in Western Arkansas in the early thirties where the Depression had struck everyone hard. My mother had her picture taken at the same time on the same boulder. She's wearing a print dress, ordinary shoes and stockings, and a little cloche hat trimmed with a strip of grosgrain ribbon.

The contrast is marked and says everything about his sense of self-importance.

The Christmas I was two, he bought me, or probably Mother bought me, an expensive Shirley Temple doll. I loved the doll because I had been to the movie theater in Booneville to see Shirley in *The Littlest Rebel*. Unfortunately, the doll wouldn't stand up to the harsh usage that I gave it. First, I messed its hair up. Then I undressed it and didn't put the dress back on.

Somehow, I broke off one of its legs. When that happened, the arm fell off too. I don't remember that I cried. I might have been too scared. How was I to know that the limbs were hooked together inside the doll's body?

My father probably wasn't in a happy mood when he came home. For some reason he noticed the doll. He became incensed. Mother was giving me a bath in the bathtub. He came storming in with the doll in one hand and a wooden ruler in the other.

He hit me on my naked thigh. My skin was wet.

I screamed. Mother screamed too, I think. I don't know whether she tried to protect me. I didn't see her face. I only saw him—his skin dark red, his eyes blazing, his mouth curling back from his teeth. He hit me again. I screamed and tried to scramble out of the other end of the tub. Perhaps Mother said something. In my utter panic and pain, I was wild to get away. I couldn't stop screaming even after he stomped out of the bathroom.

Mother wrapped me up in a towel and carried me dripping and still screaming hysterically across the yard to Mammaw's where I spent the night.

The pain stayed with me a very long time. Much longer than the welts on my skin. And I've never forgotten the expression on his face. The face of rage. Directed at a two-year-old who had broken a doll.

The other memory is even worse. One dusky summer evening Mother and I were waiting for him to come home. We heard noises on the porch. We heard a strange groaning sound just outside the door as if someone or something was in pain. My mother opened it. She didn't think to check to see who was there. She never thought to be afraid. In Booneville, Arkansas, every caller was a friend or a relative.

Outside the door was my father. He was dragging himself on his hands. His arms were at full stretch. His face was level with mine. It was contorted.

His mouth was open, and he was gasping for breath. A string of slobber dripped from his chin. I will never forget that face either.

Mother tried to push me back. She told me to go to the kitchen, but, of course, I didn't. I can still remember the horror that I couldn't understand. He was bleeding. Blood poured out of his thigh onto the floor—my mother's mopped, waxed, and polished hardwood floor. I didn't know what blood was until that instant. I didn't understand its significance.

In that instant every instinct in me reacted. I froze in horror and fear.

Before I could back away, he pulled himself into the house and tumbled down in a heap. Then he rolled over almost on my feet. Face up, he stared at me as if he didn't know who I was. He closed his mouth and wiped at it.

Mother came running back with an armful of towels. She wrapped one around his leg, then scooped me up and ran with me next door. She gave me to Mammaw again. And then she left.

I learned years later that both Doctor McConnell and Mother's cousin Elmo Stanfield, the sheriff, told her that her husband's trouser leg and the wound as well were covered with powder burns.

They were fairly certain that Fred had shot himself.

But where was the gun?

Cousin Elmo found it in the field behind the service station. Just about the distance that a strong arm could throw it from the back door. When the sheriff brought it in, my mother recognized it instantly. It was hers—the one she always kept in the top drawer of the chest-of-drawers in the bedroom.

Of course, I saw nothing of these comings and goings and incriminating discoveries. I was already asleep, safe at my grandmother's house.

πππ

When I was an adult, Dr. McConnell recalled the case very clearly and told me the whole sordid story with obvious relish. By that time, no one in Booneville liked my father, who had been cheating on my mother. He had been seeing a woman who worked at the state sanatorium on the hill above Booneville. He had bought her a diamond ring while my mother was cooking and washing dishes in a café and wearing old clothes.

Many, many years later, from a wheelchair in a nursing home, Cousin Elmo told me how he helped my mother get her grounds for divorce. My cousin wanted to set the record straight as well. Elmo picked up Mother and they drove across the Petit Jean River and up to the sanatorium. They knocked on this woman's door and found them together. I don't know whether they were *in flagrante delicto*. I wish that part of the story had been told. I wish my cousin had been more graphic about describing exactly who opened the door, what they were wearing and what they were doing. Sometimes, a girl just wants to know the whole truth.

My cousin said only that my father began to curse and rage at Mother. The sheriff had to put himself between them to protect her. Finally, Mother drove my father's car home while Fred rode with Elmo, who gave him a stern lecture and a warning.

My mother and father didn't get a divorce until a year later. After he'd cooled down, he begged her to stay with him. He promised he'd never do anything like that again. He begged for another chance.

ππ π

Since my father had burned his bridges in Booneville, we left the house my grandfather had bought for us and moved to Heavener, Oklahoma. There we lived with his parents, my grandmother whom I called Gaggy and my grandfather whom I called Tom. We lived in a rather large house. I think it had been a drummer's rooming house. It was situated beside the Kansas City Southern Railroad tracks just a walk across the yard to the end of the platform where the passengers boarded and the porters loaded the baggage. The depot was behind the garden and the stand of trees at the back of the lot.

It was all very exciting and somewhat noisy at first when the locomotives came rumbling in sounding their whistles, ringing their bells, and letting out great clouds of hissing steam.

My father went to work for the KCS and I learned to love these grandparents almost as much as my Mammaw back in Booneville. Tom, of course, was the Conductor. He was the captain of a very important passenger train named the *Southern Belle*. He had the most responsibility and his job was the nicest because he punched everyone's ticket and walked through all the cars and helped ladies on and off the trains.

There were Uncles Harve and Henry who came and went as well. They were all kind to me and I enjoyed being around them and listening to their stories of their jobs. One was an engineer I remember. One was a brakeman.

So long as my father stayed away from me, I was just fine.

Fortunately, he was working hard probably because he had no money and because he was living with his parents, who had no intention nor probably any means of buying us a house of our own.

Nevertheless, the year began one of the most idyllic of my life.

In Heavener I fell in love with horses.

My father's brother Uncle Orr, who lived up on the hill in his own house with his wife Aunt Flo, had two beautiful red horses—one bay and one sorrel—named Dan and Babe. From the very beginning, I wanted nothing so much as to ride. Instinctively, I recognized what people knew from the first time the first person mounted one—the man on horseback was the man in command. I wanted always to be in command. Somehow I believed that nothing and no-one could get me on the back of a horse.

Perhaps because I was stubborn to a fault, long-legged, and a worrywart who could pitch an screaming fit in a flash, Mother handed me up to Orr to hold in front of him while Dan walked sedately around the back yard. Soon I was begging my uncle to leave me up there while he led Dan to the saddle-barn.

Only under protest did I hold onto the horn because, as I had observed with the sharp eyes of childhood, Uncle Orr didn't hold onto the horn. He held the reins and guided Dan with them. I wanted my hands on those reins.

Everyone told me at three I was too little. Mother told me "no." Gaggy told me "no." Tom, who would have given me anything, told me "no." Orr wouldn't hear of it.

One day he left Dan standing saddled beside the back porch. The reins were looped around the horn. Quick before anyone could stop me, I threw myself onto the saddle. If I'd slipped or the horse had sidled, I'd have fallen headfirst under his hooves, but I was too determined to be afraid.

I was going to ride him. Almost in one movement, I gathered in the reins, swung them over to the left side, kicked my heels and yelled "Giddy-up!"

Dan flicked an ear back then obediently wheeled and walked away. My mother and Orr were having heart attacks, but I was never afraid for one minute. And in that instant I was determined I would never ride in front or behind anyone again.

I loved Dan with all the passion a child's heart can generate. The mahogany bay gelding stood seventeen hands. His hide was a rich red-brown. His mane and tail were midnight black. His black stockings were unblemished by white. His black nose was velvety against my palm when I fed him sugar. I treated him like a beloved pet.

I never realized how powerful he was and how highly trained.

He was the saddle horse that my uncle took to rodeos to ride in the grand parade and to rope calves. Likewise, my uncle belonged to a horseman's club that rode all over northeastern Oklahoma on weekends. Dan had the stamina and balance to carry him up and down Ouachita and Kiamichi Mountain trails.

Moreover, the gelding was a man's mount used to responding to a man's strength and a man's voice. I never knew what a chance my uncle took by letting me ride him. I wouldn't be able to control him if he took a notion to run. And if he took a notion to buck, I'd be a goner. I had nothing to hold onto. My feet wouldn't reach the stirrups. I simply refused to hold onto the horn. I wanted only the reins. I was in deadly danger every second.

Yet, in those days people didn't think about such things. They thought most people would live on farms and ranches for their whole lives long. Children had to learn to ride horses and take care of themselves around animals. The prevailing advice was, "If she gets bucked off, put her right back on, so she won't have time to think about it and be afraid."

Dan never bucked me off. Oftentimes, powerful animals, both male and female, have gentle streaks with little children. Many big dogs will let babies wool them unmercifully. Some horses will stand like statues while tots play hide-and-seek around their legs. In them domestication has achieved its highest form. Dan was one of those sterling animals.

He never so much as sidled with me in the saddle.

ππ

My grandmother Young, was a wonderful woman. She was at least five years younger than Mammaw. She and my mother were great friends. Looking back, I suspect they made the best of their situation. In exchange for a roof over our heads, Mother helped clean the house, cook the meals, do the wash, hang out of the clothes, iron the clothes, from morning till night. And what a lot there was to do for two women for four men, especially men whose jobs were essentially very dirty work.

I did nothing at all. Except be myself. Fortunately, I was cheerful. In 1937 I was the blonde blue-eyed baby darling with honeyblonde curls bouncing all over my head. My uncles were all good-looking, well-mannered men. The whole family seemed woven together without gaps dividing the generations.

Have I said that I loved Tom the best? I worshiped Tom, who would sing in a scratchy tenor voice, songs about the railroad. Of course, I learned those songs as I sang along with him.

Come all you rounders if you wanta hear
A story about a brave engineer.

I remember the songs we sang as I remember the trains at all hours, rumbling over the rails, screeching into the station, blowing off steam while they waited to unload and load passengers and baggage, clanging through all their rolling stock as they coupled and uncoupled.

The show trains put on in the stations in those days was all very impressive. Tom's *Southern Belle,* was a "flier," a deluxe passenger train. Uncle Orr and Uncle Henry were brakemen on other passenger trains and Uncle Harve was an engineer. My daddy got a job as a brakeman on a freight. Not a very glamorous job, in my opinion.

All the engines had numbers by which the dispatchers kept track of their routes, their loads, their times of departure and arrival.

Trains ran by clocks and watches. Every man carried a big gold stem-winder and setter, which he consulted at regular intervals and checked with the depot clocks. He would pull the watch from the pocket on his vest by the chain dangling across his front. At most crossings he would consult his watch. He had to be on time to that point. Meanwhile, all up and down the line, the telegraphs kept the time for the station clocks. They time was the same from Shreveport, Louisiana, to Pittsburgh, Kansas.

No one could ever be allowed to make a mistake. A few minutes slow or fast would mean disaster. Northbound trains both passengers and freights used the same tracks as southbound trains. Eastbound rumbled straight toward westbound. Moreover, a procession of northbounds, southbounds, eastbounds, and westbounds followed each other sometimes only an hour or two apart on the same lines. The possibilities for wrecks were terrifying.

The engineer ordered the firemen to regulate the speeds by putting more coal in the furnace or damping it down. The train had to be neither fast nor slow. As another safeguard when the trains approached the stations and each other, the telegraphers in the depots would wire ahead to say that such and such an eastbound was pulling out or a northbound had just passed through.

A brakeman would signal when time came for one train or the other to pull over onto a siding to let the oncoming pass. Freights pulled over for passengers; locals pulled over for the "fliers."

I loved everything about the trains. I loved most to ride them. I also loved to walk down with my grandmother or my mother to the depot to meet my daddy, my grandfather, or my uncles. I would put my bare foot on the rails and feel the iron horses coming.

I would walk back and forth, balancing on the narrow steel beam, vibrating with them. The noise would build. The three-toned whistle would shriek. The big headlight on the boiler front of the engine would flash. The smoke would streak out behind as the monster rolled into the depot.

The iron wheels, twice as tall as I was, turned in front of my very eyes. The huge drivers connecting the wheels churned back and forth. I was only a child, but I recognized the awesome power. It thrilled me to my soul.

More than once Gaggy helped me climb up, to sit in Uncle Harve's lap and stick my head out to look ahead along the massive black expanse of boiler. To be able to drive one of those as he did was the ultimate to which a boy could aspire. How I wished I were a boy!

Once in the station, the trainmen in their striped overalls and billed caps and the brakeman in his blue uniform would hurry about their business. The porters and baggage handlers would assist the passengers. My grandfather in a much fancier blue uniform with bright gold buttons and a billed hat with the KCS device over the brim would oversee everything.

At last the trainmen would signal with their lanterns—highballing to each other—from one end to the other. When the time came to pull out, my grandfather would call, "Bo-o-o-a-r-d." in the deepest, strongest voice I can ever remember. Along the line the others would answer, "All aboard."

Put in your water and shovel in your coal.

Put your head out the window, watch the drivers roll.

It all fascinated me. It was our family. I thought my father would be an engineer or even a conductor too someday. I looked forward to his success.

πππ

Then the message came that changed everything. I wasn't present when my grandmother received it. I only heard the weeping. Mother hurried down to be with her. Aunt Florence, Uncle Henry's wife came and stayed. Aunt Flo, Uncle Orr's young wife, came over and then went away.

Headaches and heartaches and all kinds of pain

Are ever a part of the railroad train.

I sat still on the floor out of the way while the women sat together and touched and held each other. And I listened.

Soon others began to arrive. Heavener had a roundhouse that turned engines around and headed them back up the tracks. Many railroad men and their wives lived there. Every wife knew and dreaded my grandmother's tragedy.

The northbound freight had run into the back of another northbound.

The engine, Harve's engine, had crashed through the caboose as if it were kindling and jumped the track. It became every trainman's nightmare, a thundering juggernaut, the greatest force man had then created—a runaway train.

The fireman jumped off, the brakeman and conductor jumped out of the caboose, but Harve stayed with it to the end, riding the brakes, fighting the steel horses until the monster had run into a culvert and turned over.

Deeds that are honest and noble and grand
Belong in the life of a railroad man.

Harve was thrown from the cab into the ditch. The boiler cracked. Surrounded by live steam, he couldn't find his way out. He was scalded.

He was still alive, but there was no hope. The flesh was literally falling off his body. He would die in a hospital a hundred miles up the track. My grandmother would never see him again.

The worst thing of all was that the accident had been caused by a mistake. A man had looked at his watch wrong. He mistook a big hand for a little hand in the dark. He didn't switch his train off the track fast enough. The man was my uncle Orr.

My grandmother's elder son had caused the death of her baby brother. How could a woman live with such pain? How could any person man or woman live knowing he had caused the death of another family member, someone he had loved?

Uncle Orr was suspended for a year without pay. In the midst of the depression, he and Aunt Flo suffered.

Daddy quit the railroad entirely. Work like that was dangerous. He worked at odd jobs in Heavener, but never anything with any future. Perhaps there was nothing to be had. With time on his hands, he started trifling on my mother again, so she left him.

We went to the Valley where months would go by before I even heard a distant whistle.

I never missed my daddy. In fact, I never thought about him. I longed to see Gaggy and Tom. I thought about Uncle Orr, Uncle Henry, and Uncle Harve, whom I realized in some awful way I would never, never see again.

I missed Dan.

And I missed the trains. Whenever we walked across the railroad tracks in Raymondville, I would step on the rails and walk along them as far as I could. Sometimes I'd feel vibrations singing through the iron from far, far away. They made me want to laugh and cry at the same time.

They were the only tangible memories I had of a happy time. To this day, I cannot merely step across a railroad track. I have to walk it.

IV
THE FARM

The Valley was a singular place to grow up. Its two dozen or so little towns and hamlets were isolated from the rest of Texas and the United States by the feudal fiefdom known as the King Ranch. The huge cattle kingdom of nearly a million acres had been carved out of land no one wanted. The Texans called it Wild Horse Desert. The Mexicans called it *El Desierto de los Muertos*, The Desert of the Dead.

In the nineteenth century Captain Richard King had seen it as wealth where he could raise a steer for two dollars and sell it at the railhead in Abilene, Kansas, for eighteen. To raise those cattle, King had to fight off rustlers from both sides of the Rio Grande. When he died of cancer, his widow continued the fight.

From the beginning of the twentieth century Henrietta King, *La Patrona*, and her son-in-law Robert Kleberg had used the Valley as a buffer between the ranch and the bandits from Old Mexico.

The Valley was fifty miles wide by over a hundred long. The Gulf of Mexico was its eastern boundary and the Rio Grande bounded it on the south and west. The powerful family kept it cut off from the rest of the United States except by the railroad that they had themselves decided was in their best interests to ship their cattle to market rather than drive them through farmlands and hostile farmers to the railheads in Kansas. The St. Louis, Brownsville, and Matamoros ran 141 miles from Robstown west of Corpus Christi. It made its first run July 4, 1904. Not till many decades later did the U. S. Highway Department manage to cleave a right-of-way through it.

The King Ranch owners did not see the need for another highway running south to Brownsville. The Military Highway south from San Antonio some twenty-five miles west was more than sufficient. Finally U. S. Highway 77 was built and to this day runs seventy-five miles due south paralleling the rails of the old Brownie replaced by the much newer Missouri-Pacific. Both the iron rails and the concrete strip were lined on both sides by barbed wire fence.

Driving was not encouraged. When my mother and I came to the Valley in 1938, there was no gasoline to be bought between Kingsville, where the historic ranch had its headquarters, and Raymondville. *Los Kineños,* the sons and grandsons of Richard King's Mexican *vaqueros,* rode along it in chaps and sombreros with six shooters on their hips and rifles in their saddle-boots.

When Judge Gill and Mr. Rollo Harding began to develop the land and sell it in 254, 508, and 635-acre tracts, my grandfather heard about it and bought two tracts. They were pieces of undeveloped land.

Below the barrier of the King Ranch, virgin brush country had somehow escaped most of the civilizing influences of the twentieth century. South of it lay fertile delta land previously unfarmed at the mouth of one of America's great rivers whose headwaters had their origins in the snows of the Colorado Rockies and whose mouth was the Gulf of Mexico.

The Valley itself was a miracle.

A man with a desire for sport could shoot a whitetail buck from his back porch. A fisherman could pull freshwater tropical fish from the delta's tributaries and the Gulf's fingers. A saltwater fisherman could drop a line is the long lagoon between Padre Island and the Texas coastline and haul out redfish and speckled trout in seconds.

The names given to all this water—Laguna Madre, Resaca de los Fresnos, and Arroyo Colorado—were foreign to our ears.

The population was small and sparse. The town of Raymondville had no more than four or five streets. Fewer than one hundred fifty people and businesses had telephones in the whole of Willacy County.

East of town stood a general store at a crossroads designated on the maps as Santa Margarita. It was run by a man named Meade, who looked like an old cowboy from the Wild West. He had a little white goatee and long white hair that flowed over his shoulders.

He made me think of Buffalo Bill. He also kept horehound drops in a big glass apothecary jar beside the cash register. When we'd pay, he'd hand me a piece of hard candy to suck on the way home.

"What do you say?" my grandmother would ask.

"Thank you, Mr. Meade." Then, my manners minded, I'd pop it into my mouth. I didn't particularly like horehound. It was a kind of mint that people boiled to make cough drops, but it was somewhat sweet like candy, so I sucked it dutifully

As I remember, his store was open at any time, for we would go there after Mother got home at full dark. We raised almost all our vegetables, kept chickens for meat, and cows for milk, but we purchased certain necessities—flour, corn meal, dried beans, sugar, and the like.

Meade was a true Valley pioneer who boasted a long history of defending himself and his property against intruders. It was well known that he kept several pistols hidden about the store.

His neighbors and customers gossiped about the time he'd actually sold a sack of dried pinto beans with a Derringer amongst them. Somehow he'd scooped up the beans with his big scoop and not noticed the little popgun.

The person who'd got the weapon returned it for more beans and the story spread. Everyone laughed about it. They held him in highest respect and thought he was quite a fellow.

His store didn't really have much for sale. In the middle of the floor were some sturdy oak tables with shirts and overalls and Panama straw hats displayed on them. He generally stood by his cash register behind his single counter. A few canned goods were lined up on shelves behind him. All a customer had to do was ask, and he'd hand anything over.

We would give him our list and he'd make up the order while Mammaw and Mother talked with Mrs. Meade. His flour and sugar came in fifty-pound sacks with calico prints. His dried beans and peas were stocked in barrels.

A big Lady Grace pickle jar sat on the opposite end of the counter from the cash register. I remember those huge pale yellow-green pickles. They were so sour that one bite would pinch my mouth tight as a penny purse. He stocked apples in a two-sectioned box and soda crackers in a big tin.

Someone told me many, many years later that he also made whiskey that he kept in jugs behind the counter. He sold it only to certain preferred customers. My mother wouldn't have asked for it anyway. My grandmother was very strict about what was brought into the house. We were strictly reared in the precepts of the Methodist Church.

The story was told that a terrible thing happened to him. Mother was terribly afraid after she heard it and Mammaw and she discussed how this might effect them. For that reason it remains so clearly in my mind along with his long white hair and his black suspenders over his white collarless shirts.

Across the border came Mexican bandits with long memories and a desire to emulate Juan Cortinas, the nineteenth century outlaw, rustler, and murderer who hated the people from the United States of America whom he called *Tejanos*.

They galloped up to Meade's store and looted the cash register. When they didn't find enough to suit them, they demanded more. Meade said he didn't have any more. Unfortunately, they knew better. He was also rumored to have large caches of money hidden.

They hit him across the face. Then one of them started to strangle Mrs. Meade. I suspect that they were going to rape her, but, of course, such atrocities weren't spoken of in the presence of four-year-old children.

When his wife started screaming and crying, the fierce old man struggled to his feet and went for one of the several pistols hidden around the store. The robbers caught him and shot him with his own gun. Then they took their loot and escaped taking Mrs. Meade with them. .

I was upset to hear about it. I retreated to the topmost boughs of the salt cedars, where I could think and plan my course of action should such a thing happen to me.

I was really sorry to hear that the store closed and the Santa Margarita crossroads passed into history. We had to drive into Raymondville thereafter where the grocery stores were much less interesting.

I don't know whether my mother ever discussed another possibility with my grandmother. Perhaps there was another story.

Why would a gang of Mexican bandits ride fifty miles north from the river to rob a lonely store? Why not rob the grocery store in Raymondville itself where there was much more money not much better protected?

The other story that I have heard is that Mrs. Meade was not Mrs. Meade at all. She was the wife of another man, a Mexican rancher, who lived in a big house in northwestern Kenedy County. He was a ruthless man who treated her badly, so she left him and ran to Meade who promised to protect her.

When he discovered where she was, he sent his men to bring her back. When Meade tried to protect her, they killed him.

No one will ever know the true story. A man had a right to keep his wife from another man. If Mr. Meade wasn't her husband, then he was "asking for it." Perhaps the easiest thing was to consider that rough justice had been done.

In the bad old days of the Valley, problems were often settled without resorting to the law.

I didn't think about what a dangerous place we were living in. I didn't know that my mother kept her own gun cleaned and loaded. It was the one that my father had used to shoot himself. She was ready for action as was every other adult in the Valley.

I have a hard time picturing my mother with a deadly Colt in her fist. She was so civilized, so refined, such a lady. But looking back, I think she could have sighted down that gun-barrel at an intruder and pulled that trigger without a second's hesitation.

We women were so vulnerable there on that farm with only the hired man in his house out back. Our closest neighbors were Ira Page and Alfred

Pennington, men with wives and daughters who were just as vulnerable as we were.

The small towns where we traded were miles away. Probably no more than a dozen law officers covered the four counties.

But if we'd all been wiped out, other farmers would have come inevitably, inexorably, because the land was so good, so very fertile, so very hospitable to crops.

The Valley would draw people like us because farming was what we did, how we made our living. We'd find it and make it ours.

My quarter section—254 acres—from my grandfather, to my grandmother, to my mother, to me, and someday to my daughter is what I am. No matter how hard times may get, I'll never sell it. Always, I've owned a farm.

πππ

In the Valley every plant grew at a phenomenal rate. When farmers planted carrots or onions, they grew to maturity in five to seven weeks. They made a feast for dozens of varieties of birds as well as rabbits, hares, possums, ground squirrels, and all manner of omnivorous varmints. Where they ranged, carnivorous animals followed.

How to keep our chickens from getting eaten by predators was one of Mammaw's constant problems.

Chickens could and did range free and forage for themselves. To be sure they'd come home at night, Mammaw would scatter a small pan of feed for them each evening—just to let them know where their home was.

The larger animals like the pigs and the beef and dairy cows were always kept in pens and pastures because the damage they could do to a field of grain or corn was too great to be borne. A herd of milk cows in a cornfield could eat up the profits in a day. Only after the corn had been harvested, did we turn them into the stubble fields. In this way, nothing was wasted.

But chickens didn't need to be penned because they couldn't do any damage. On the other hand, if they stayed outside at night, they would lay their eggs where they slept and both hens and eggs would make a meal for predatory animals. Coyotes and bobcats like chicken just as much as rabbit, especially because they're easier to catch and kill. Skunks would eat eggs three times a day if they could get them.

I knew all this and felt no sympathy for the poor clucks. I never made pets of the chickens. Who would want to? They couldn't be petted very well. Their scaly feet and toes got in the way. They didn't have sense enough to be afraid, so they didn't have sense enough to be affectionate either. A child in a storybook who made a pet of a chicken must have been a very lonely child indeed.

Today I never notice animal rights activists marching to save chickens from abuse, even though they're much more abused and much more worthy than stinky, ill-tempered minks or foxes. Sad but true, chickens arouse no one's sympathies.

As a matter of fact, they were really almost the perfect domestic food source. Little was discarded except the feathers and the entrails. We ate the eggs until the hens stopped laying. Then we ate the hens. From time to time Mammaw would allow clutches of eggs to hatch, and the process would began again in a very few months.

They might have aroused more sympathy if they hadn't been so incredibly nasty about their habits. Their droppings were everywhere because, though they scratched industriously, unlike cats, they didn't have sense enough to cover their mess. I had to wash my bare feet many times at the outdoor faucet. Ugh!

Whenever Mammaw would order a big flat box of one hundred baby chickens, usually Leghorns or Rhode Island Reds, from Sears, Roebuck, I'd cup the cute little yellow fuzzballs in my hands for a few minutes, then go off to play in the salt cedars. I knew that in a very short time pinfeathers would begin to appear on their wings and tails. Then longer feathers would sprout in ugly clumps all over their bodies. Then they'd be grown. When Mammaw caught one and wrung its head off, I'd watch the body jump around with only mild interest. They weren't *ever* pets.

When the chicks grew big enough to be turned out to range for themselves, they didn't know where they belonged, so they'd try to roost in the salt cedars. Mammaw would send me up to roust them. I'd flap my arms and shake the branches until they flew down, cackling and squawking. Then together she and I would shoo them into the henhouse.

Every time Mammaw ordered chickens, the farm seemed to be overrun with skunk, opossum, raccoon, coyote, and even bobcat—all stealing meals. We'd hear a terrific squawking, then see a flash of white. Some stupid fowl hiding out in the grain, vegetables, or cotton had been found by a predator and made off with.

Besides not knowing where their homes are, chickens are too stupid to know where to lay their eggs. Mammaw would fix nests for them in the henhouse, but they'd lay in the fields where chicken snakes and black snakes would be sure to get the eggs.

To encourage the chickens to come to the right place, Mammaw bought some pretty milk-glass eggs to put in the nests. They didn't look much like real eggs, being pale blue and translucent.

But could the hens tell the difference? Not at all. They'd think a glass egg was their egg from the day before. They'd think they themselves had been there and would settle down to lay another egg beside it.

Wouldn't you think a mother would know the difference in fake and real children?

Unlike good little girls in pastoral stories, I never liked to gather eggs. Broody hens are vicious. One of them pecked me hard enough to draw blood from my arm. After that I steered clear. Mammaw wore gloves and one of Pawpaw's long-sleeved shirts when she gathered the eggs.

Once I got too close when several hens were setting. The rooster who was the father of the brood attacked me. He ran at me, flapping his wings and screeching. Not a yard in front of me, he hopped into the air and flew at me with talons hooked to spur my leg.

I screamed and kicked fiercely. "Get away, you goddam rooster!"

I kicked him again, but he came back and actually drew blood before Mammaw could get after him with the broom. She took me into the house and cleaned the wound very carefully. Though it was just a scratch, she knew the talons were covered with barnyard filth.

Then she scolded me for using bad words. I was reminded, in case I had forgotten, that I was going to be a lady when I grew up. Ladies did not use bad language.

One night we had a visitor in the henhouse—a big blacksnake—longer than I was tall. We knew he must have been smart enough to crawl up the walkway and slide in under the screen door because when Mammaw found him, he was trying to get out the same way he'd come in.

Only he couldn't.

Snakes are worthy adversaries for chickens. They are evenly matched in intelligence. Neither can tell the difference between real and fake eggs. The blacksnake had swallowed three of Mammaw's milk-glass ones.

His body with the egg lumps inside was then too thick to pass under the door. He kept trying to get away, but he didn't have sense enough to pull back when Mammaw came out and saw him.

She ran for the hoe and, amidst squawking and much fluttering of feathers, she dragged him out and chopped off his head. A well-sharpened hoe blade—six inches wide and five inches deep on the end of five feet of seasoned ash wood—is a formidable weapon when wielded by a determined woman. Even though the snake was over four feet long, he never stood a chance.

Everybody came out in time to see his headless body writhing in great whipping circles on the ground. We weren't afraid. We weren't in awe. Mammaw had successfully dispatched a predator. That was part and parcel of living seven miles from town.

None of us was even repulsed by what she did next. Indeed, Mother and Mammaw merely grimaced at each other. I watched wide-eyed.

My grandmother took up the hoe again and chopped the writhing body into three parts—and mucked out her glass eggs. She washed them under the faucet in the backyard and put them back in the nests. The hens climbed back in, settled their feathers around them, and got back to business.

They weren't even smart enough to scared.

How my grandmother's delicate sensibilities must have been revolted! She had earned a high school diploma with studies in music and Latin. She had written a philosophic paper titled "Sunshine and Shadow." She had been a banker's daughter and a wealthy man's wife. She had lived in a two-story house on the best street in her hometown. She had owned a black silk-velvet coat with a black mink collar, a coat Rachel and I share today to wear to operas and ballets. Less than five years had passed since she'd had all those things.

That morning she must have put them all aside—firmly pushed them back into a corner of her mind and locked them away. We were living on the land. The land must be made to give all it can.

Three glass eggs meant three real eggs laid beside them, collected, and eaten for breakfast the next day. Protein to make me strong and tall. Protein to sustain our lives.

The power of my grandmother amazed me then. Now I stand in absolute awe of her fortitude and courage.

$$\pi\pi\pi$$

A farm is dangerous place. In order to work it profitably, a man has tractors—huge vehicles with great power and almost no safety devices. The power is necessary to pull a variety of plows, cultivators, and harvesters all of which have served time and again as inspirations for death machines in third, second, and first rate horror films.

Safety devices seem unnecessary since a tractor doesn't move very fast. But many a farmer has been killed when the slow-moving, clumsy machine has turned over or kept on running when he's been bucked off the small, high metal seat.

As a little girl, I was kept strictly away from all those things. But there was no way to keep me away from the pieces of jagged aluminum, steel, and iron filings, the snippets of baling wire, the nails, the screws, the thousand bits of unforgiving metal that littered the area around the barns and sheds.

Even if Mammaw started me out with shoes on, I took them off as soon as climbed into the salt cedars and left them off for the rest of the day.

The balls of my feet, the pads of my toes, the cushions of my heels were hard as shoe leather, but not my arches. Unfortunately, my feet had high arches, a gift from some English ancestor, my grandmother said. More than half my foot never bore weight on the ground. That is to say, it skimmed a barest fraction of an inch above it. It was a prime target for the metallic shards.

Mother took me for a tetanus shot soon after I came to the Valley. Mammaw washed my feet and lectured me about the danger of lockjaw, a truly dreadful disease, that so many farmers and their children died of back when Mammaw was young before tetanus had been discovered and a preventive shot developed. Still I wouldn't wear my shoes.

And I was healthy as a goat.

When I'd get a cut or puncture, my grandmother had a favorite remedy that undoubtedly accounted for my salvation to this day. It was known to people from the rural areas of the country as "coal oil." Kerosene, kept in tins and jugs and lamp wells in every home in America before electricity became readily available, was what her father used to sterilize any wound she might have gotten.

The first time I remember her using it, I had been up to my usual tricks. I had leaped before I looked. I had jumped out of the salt cedars onto a board with not one but two crooked rusty nails sticking out of it. I had been using the board to draw parallel lines in the dirt and had left it lying beneath the tree. Thus I'd brought about my own disaster—as I usually did.

Blood was gushing from my arch. I was scared enough to run screaming for Mammaw.

She sat me down on a straight chair and brought a pan of warm water into which she'd poured a little salt. It must not have been enough to sting because I don't remember that it did. Carefully she bathed my foot, dried it off, and inspected it.

I had to twist my sole around to see too. The wounds weren't really deep at all.

What a disappointment after all that blood!

Mammaw had me press a clean towel against the place while she prepared the bandage. She tore a strip off a clean rag, poured coal oil on it and wrapped it tightly around my foot. I don't remember anything hurting after that.

I was ready to go back out. But she wouldn't let me. I had to lie down on the daybed on the screened back porch for the rest of the day with my injured foot cocked on the knee of the other leg.

I could read. I could color. I could embroider a dresser-scarf (not likely). I could go to the bathroom. Otherwise, I was to stay put.

The next morning, it was all healed. Not just scabbed over, but closed. The holes were just red bruised spots but with no sign of real infection.

I thought nothing at all about this miracle of medicine though now I think Mammaw should have published in the *Journal of the American Medical Association*. All I knew then was that my grandmother did it. It was the proper thing to do. It worked.

Of course, I'd had my tetanus shot. And the bleeding probably cleansed the wound. The salt water would have cleaned my skin. The clean rag and the quiet rest could have done its work. But I believed it was the coal oil.

From that day on, whenever I came in with blood gushing, dripping, or trickling from a wound in the arch of my foot, Mammaw would wash it and wrap it in a rag soaked in coal oil. The full treatment never varied except that after Rural Electrification, I could listen to the radio. And like magic it would be healed in just a day.

My grandmother could do absolutely anything.

Anything!

$$\pi\pi\pi$$

Suffice to say I grew up with wild creatures all around and even on the farm. The 254-acre quarter section hadn't even been completely cleared when we moved onto it. Coyotes sang their songs to each other sometimes so close they seemed at the backdoor. Our farm had two lagoons where brackish water collected. Mesquite trees, grasses of all kind, and even cactus grew there, thick and virtually impenetrable.

These lagoons were filled with what the Mexicans called *brasada*. So destructive was this brush that *vaqueros* wore bull-hide chaps when they had to ride through it. Even the withers and forelegs of their horses were fitted with the same sort of contrivances. Possum, skunk, and raccoon nightly made their treks across the plowed fields and through the crops to nose around my grandmother's hen house, the pigpens, the silo, and any other places where they could steal a meal.

The fields were alive with cottontails and jackrabbits. The smaller, the little cottontails, the true rabbits, were everywhere. Our black tractor driver John brought me one from time to time when he'd stir up a burrow or nest with his plow. They were always babies not really old enough to leave their mothers.

We'd put greens in their little makeshift pens for a few days, but somehow they always got away. Never once did I suspect that Mammaw let the cottontails out. She wouldn't deny me a few days pleasure, but she didn't want to rabbits to die either. She was the most tender-hearted woman I ever knew.

Jackrabbits—true hares—were bigger than cottontails. They had monstrous long ears and powerful long legs. They were rarer or perhaps just faster. We'd see them jump across the road sometimes, but I'd never seen one up close. I'd certainly never held one.

Then one day John brought me a baby jackrabbit. It was twice as big as the cottontails. Its powerful hind legs with long claws scrabbled and kicked at the air. Its long ears rose and flattened against its back as it tried to escape.

"Hold it tight," he said. "It'll get away."

I didn't know any better. I closed my two hands around its body and held it as tight as I could. Its little heart beat beneath my fingers. Its little lungs tried to expand.

Then its head fell limply to one side. All four legs relaxed at once.

I had killed it.

To this day when I write about this small, terrible thing, I want somehow to undo it. I'm so ashamed. I didn't mean to. I couldn't know.

But I knew what I was. I had read enough fairy tales to know. I was a stupid giant child. I was an ogre. And nobody had stolen my golden goose either. I couldn't even say, "Fe-fi-fo-fum."

I stared at the little body. I shook it. I let it go. It lay like a thin brown skin unmoving.

I wept. Mammaw had to hold me even though I wasn't a baby any longer. Together we buried it although I wasn't much help. I cried so hard that Mammaw had to take it out of my hands and put it in the little hole she'd dug at the end of cotton row. I covered it over with salt cedar boughs and prayed, "Now I lay me down to sleep."

It was the only prayer I knew and every word cut me to the quick.

The next time John brought me a rabbit, I let it go immediately. I'd lost the desire for wild animals of any kind. Even to this day, the confession that I killed that jackrabbit is like confessing to murder. That accidental act has given me an unalterable guilt to live with, a sin for which I can't ever atone.

Thereafter, when Pastor Cox at the Methodist Church talked about a guilty conscience, I knew what he meant. Stronger even than his sermons were my grandmother's admonitions. And now they all had teeth. I understood that I had done something terrible and that what I had done was irrevocable. I was afraid that I might do something like that again.

Dimly, I realized why my grandmother was trying so hard to make me be good. She didn't want me to be a wild child who pitched terrible temper tantrums and smashed and hurt things. She didn't want me to be Fred Young's daughter. She wanted me to be a good girl who would grow up to be a good woman.

When my grandmother lectured me, I listened more carefully than I had before. When she asked, "Aren't you ashamed of yourself, Mona Dean?" I almost always was.

Sometimes while she was ironing or doing some other chore, she would talk about my being on the side of the right and the just. She worked education into her lectures by insisting that I must be smart—I must study hard and learn everything I could so I would know right from wrong and make the wise choices.

She made me what I am. I can't imagine what sort of person I would be, if she hadn't been so wise.

πππ

Farms endure all kinds of plagues. When we learned in Sunday School about the Seven Plagues of Egypt, no one in the First Methodist Church South in Raymondville thought much about them.

Moses probably knew he didn't really have anything special to say. He knew all about Pharaoh because he'd lived in the palace himself and realized that the Lord of the Two Kingdoms and Conqueror of the Hittites hadn't been out and about in the countryside. If he had been, he would have known that things like frogs and grasshoppers happened every year.

Frogs were nothing. They didn't eat the crops. Indeed, we had a migration of frogs one year. The rains had been especially heavy. One day tiny thumb-sized gray-green frogs appeared everywhere—in the yard, in the fields, in the road. The school bus ran over them and squashed them flat.

I caught them by the dozens despite my grandmother's warnings. "You'll get warts."

I believed her, but I was sure I could avoid touching them. I hemmed them in with wide pieces of tin and dumped them in jars.

I put flour on them so they'd be white and turned them loose. Why that seemed like something to do, I have no idea. I dug a wide hole deep enough to keep them from jumping out. I put them in it and made a deeper smaller hole in the bottom of it. I filled it with water, so they'd have a pond to swim in. They kept me busy for days. I didn't get a wart until years later, but when I showed it to her, she said, "There. You see. I told you not to play with frogs."

If Pharaoh thought locusts were bad, he should have had to fight the pests that we fought as a matter of course every year.

One year we planted onions only to have them ruined by onion thrips. Of course, Moses wouldn't have called those down to make Pharaoh let the people go because the Supreme Ruler of the Nile couldn't really see them.

He could only see where they'd been. Millions of tiny white dots of dead tissue on the onion tops until the plant simply wilted onto the ground, and the bulb beneath it didn't develop. Enough of them destroyed the entire field.

Just about the ugliest creature is the tobacco hornworm. Pharaoh must have known about it. It's sometimes three or four inches long and it looks ferocious. It's an eating machine that rears up on its hind legs and bluffs whenever it feels threatened. Otherwise, it looks like a curled version of the leaf or cotton boll or vegetable or whatever it's eating. What it will do to the interior of a bright red sun-warmed tomato doesn't bear repeating.

I used to play at crushing the hornworms between bricks. They'd splash into great pea green globs of leaf matter and chlorophyll.

Moses missed a good bet not bringing down a plague of those. Besides being enormously destructive, they were truly hideous enough to frighten anyone but a farm-reared child.

In most years when circumstances were ordinary, red-winged blackbirds would eat enough of them to spare us severe damage, but one year we had a real infestation so the blackbirds couldn't handle the job.

In the nineteenth century on the old plantations, the hornworms were pulled off the plants by hand, doused with kerosene, and burned. Of course, we didn't have the money to hire a crew to do that. We had to use poison that also cost a lot of money. It meant we wouldn't make as much on our crop.

Pharaoh was just lucky that the Egyptian cotton didn't get boll weevils. That's a real plague. Or root rot where whole acreages turn black. One year the problems of boll weevils, root rot, and drought combined to virtually destroy everyone's crop. For us the toll was two hundred fifty acres of Sea Island Long Staple cotton planted with such hope for the future and then irretrievably lost. My grandmother made $800 that year. Taxes alone were $1200.

If Pharaoh thought Moses' plague of thunder, fire, and hail was terrible, he should have lived in the Valley when a hurricane blew in. The sky would turn purple at noon. The wind would flatten everyone's fields of grain and cotton. Then the rain would flood the fields and drown what lay on the ground.

In fact, as I remember the one thing Pharaoh did understand was that everyone in Egypt was affected by the destruction of crops. And so was everyone in the Valley.

My grandmother was reduced to cutting up my mother's old dresses and skirts to make me new clothes. This meant that C. R. Anthony, Terry-Farris, and Addington's clothing stores didn't make sales to us. Of course, we didn't buy new cars from Welch Chevrolet. We didn't buy as many groceries. We put off repairs on our houses. We made do. And so did anyone else in town.

See that, Pharaoh! That's what a real disaster's all about.

Why would anyone embark on such a terrible profession as farming? Because of all the professions in the world, it's the most basic. It's the sun and the rain and the sweat and the dirt and the knowledge that cotton and corn and cabbage and grain and carrots and onions and sugar cane begin on your land and go all around the world.

It's another reason why we've never sold the farm.

πππ

When we were getting ready to leave Oklahoma and move to the Valley, my mother told me all about the friend I'd have to play with. Mother said she had curls just like I did except hers were brown. She would play dolls with me and we would share secrets. She lived just next door and we would play together all the time. Her name was Ruth Warren.

Mother also said that I must start minding my manners and stop pitching temper tantrums and yelling and screaming when I couldn't have my way. Ruth was older than I was and wouldn't like me if I behaved like a baby.

I thought often and hard about my mother's instructions. I tried very hard to heed them, but I'm afraid I failed more than a few times. When I grew frustrated or didn't get my way, I was Fred Young's daughter to the life.

Nevertheless, shortly after we arrived, Harley and Lillian Warren came to visit and welcome my mother and brought Ruth with them. She was exquisite. Not that at four, I knew the word exquisite. I only knew that she was all my mother had said and more. She was the same size as I was, but she was so beautiful. Because she was nearly a year and a half older than I, she seemed infinitely more mature. She had such lovely manners and her knees weren't all scabbed over.

She was the youngest of four children. I didn't know then that she was my age while Lillian and Harley were the same age as my grandmother. I believe her oldest brother David had already married and gone while Ned, the brother closest to her, used to go out honky-tonking with my Uncle Jack. Sometimes Aunt Jane went too, but most times she didn't even know they'd gone.

Likewise, I didn't get to know her older sister until many years later. Laurene came with her mother and sister to visit one day. I was up in the salt cedars as usual. I let out a Tarzan shriek as I swung down. She looked at me as though I'd lost my mind and went into the house to sit with Mammaw and Mrs. Warren. Ruth and I were left to play as we chose. I came to understand that Laurene was in high school and much too busy being one of the prettiest and smartest girls in Raymondville to pay much attention to us babies.

The Warren family did live next door but not the way that people did in Booneville or Heavener. In the way of country homesteads, considerable distances down country lanes stretched from door to door. Consequently, we children didn't spend long playtimes together. I didn't eat breakfast and hop on my tricycle to pedal down to Ruth's house, a bare half mile away. I didn't pedal around anywhere except my own dirt driveway and my backyard.

Even though a dog could sleep undisturbed in the road beneath the salt cedars from the time the school bus rumbled by in the morning till it came back by in the afternoon, Mammaw would no more have let me out of that yard unsupervised than she would have sold me to a band of gypsies.

I might swing wildly through those trees and gallop barefoot around the yard. I might play hide and seek by myself out around the barn and the sheds, but Mammaw had imposed invisible fences. I knew the boundaries well.

So did Ruth.

We only visited when her mother came to visit Mammaw or we went to visit them. Since neither one of them had a car to drive, visiting would have required them to walk down dirt roads. Such a possibility never occurred to either of them. They were ladies. Dirt roads were not for strolling.

Moreover, both had a prodigious number of chores to do everyday. Lillian had five or six family members. She had a full time job to keep them clean and fed and picked up after.

Mammaw had only Mother and me, but she also had her bad arm and weak side, the results of a radical mastectomy to cure her of breast cancer. She was still recovering and had to sit down and rest in the afternoons.

Visiting for us girls was a special occasion.

I've said I admired Ruth. Worship would be more like the feelings she engendered. In my own mind I suffered so by comparison. She was beautiful with long brown hair. My hair was short and dishwater blonde. She was dainty. I stumbled over my own feet.

We played dolls together. She had a Shirley Temple, I think. I had a Snow White dressed just like the character in the Disney movie. I had a padded doll trunk made from a sturdy orange crate. It held dozens of doll clothes Mammaw made out of scraps of my own dress materials.

But I was so envious of Ruth's dollhouse. Her father Harley was a carpenter. He'd made it out of real wood. From the front and sides it looked just like a real house. It had no back, so she could sit behind it and place the dolls and their furniture in the various rooms. It even had a staircase to the second floor. He'd painted the roof green and fastened green shutters on either. It was beautiful. Only in the case of that dollhouse did I know real envy.

I've never gotten over the fact that she loaned the dollhouse to a cousin who never returned it. Somehow it wasn't *all* hers to lend.

As for her talent, I didn't begrudge her that. It was so prodigious that I couldn't even imagine being like her. She could play beautiful music on the piano with her fingers. I played the player piano with my feet. While she was performing Chopin, I was stomping out "Yes, We Have No Bananas."

Later when we took lessons from Mrs. B. S. Wright, I always played at the beginning of the piano recitals. As every piano student knows and suffers agonies of embarrassment over, the less accomplished the player, the closer to the beginning of the evening she plays.

This order gets the torturous but mercifully short pieces over early and allows the evening to end with real music. Ruth always came near the end or dead last. She didn't stay with Mrs. B. S. Wright long. She switched to the most accomplished teacher in the Valley. Hers was the real gift for music. I did well to play a scale and carry a tune.

It never occurred to me to be jealous. Like a neophyte worshipping a goddess, I worshipped her. My mother had told me I would like her. And like her I did although I didn't really have any secrets to tell her then.

I'm sure Harley was disappointed that he didn't get to build the big house that Pawpaw had brought him down from Arkansas to build. The day came when he told Mammaw he was moving. He had found a small house for his family to live in while he built people's new houses as Raymondville grew.

I was wretched when Mammaw told me that Ruth would be moving into town. She assured me, however, that we'd still get to play because she would be visiting them nearly as often. I had to be satisfied with that.

Except for the grade when I went to Willamar, Ruth and I were always in school together in the same room. Since her name was Warren and mine was Young, we sat one behind the other in alphabetical order through junior high. We read the same books. Our mothers subscribed to the Junior Literary Guild for us. We attended the Methodist Church together and sang in the choir. She sang a beautiful alto. Because I was never able to train my ear to hear anything but the top note, I had to sing a poor soprano without the range for it.

We graduated in the same class and drove off to colleges in Denton, Texas, together. Ruth went to North Texas State to major in music and I went to Texas State College for Women to major in English. We frequently rode home together on the same bus.

.

My grandmother is gone now. Our mothers and fathers as well. Her brothers are both dead as are Aunt Jane and Uncle Jack, recently, the last leaf.

Through the years we've lived in difference places, but we always manage to visit face to face at least once a year. Thank heaven we've never been farther apart than the telephone because now we have real secrets to tell each other. Some are sad. Some are wonderful. Our children are moving on toward middle age and Ruth is a grandmother twice over.

She's always been there for me, never far from my thoughts, always a present memory. I can't think what I would have done without her.

V
FAMILY PROBLEMS

I hated to leave Gaggy and Tom, but once in the Valley I climbed my first salt cedar. With the fickleness or adaptability of childhood, I had an entirely new interest.

My mother never let me know how unhappy and ashamed she was, nor how her problems often seemed insurmountable. What she hadn't counted on was facing censure for not preserving her bad marriage. She didn't realize she would be looked down on and her reputation as a lady and a good woman would be besmirched. That came later.

In Raymondville Mother got an uncontested divorce. It provided that my father could come to visit me, but he could never take me away with him. Mother didn't ask for child support. As she told me when I asked about it as an adult, "I couldn't get blood out of a turnip."

Perhaps my father was right in never coming to visit me because I certainly never missed him. Life on the farm was too exciting. Most of the time, I was galloping around on stick horses, swinging through the salt cedars, and screaming for the sheer joy of hearing my own voice.

If we had been able to stay isolated on the farm, if we hadn't had to go into town, life would have been paradise.

Or if he had cared enough about me to come just once, he could have saved my mother and me so much pain.

My mother and father were DIVORCED. People censured divorce in those days. Almost no one was divorced. A divorced woman was an outcast in a society that judged the breakup of her marriage as her fault. Frequently, she was shunned as fast and loose. Other women didn't offer friendship because that "hussy" might want someone else's husband.

The general attitude of others made my mother's situation much worse than if she had been a widow. She might have starved in genteel poverty, but she would have had friends. Since she was divorced, she could starve and no one would even befriend her. A rumor flitted around that she had never been married. That made me something terrible too. Fortunately, I didn't know what. The word was too shocking for nice people to utter.

My mother couldn't stay hidden on the farm. We were land poor. We needed money. So she went out to find a job. No local merchant would hire anyone with her unacceptable reputation. Only the telephone company with its headquarters elsewhere in another county, another state, another world was hiring anyone. It was having trouble finding operators because going to work in front of a machine was like going to work in a factory. Nice ladies didn't do such things. Moreover, telephone operators had bad reputations.

How she was driven to the telephone company is perhaps the most tragic story of her life. I didn't even realize how much she was hurting or what a trial I was going to have to live through.

Mother had enjoyed the benefits of a fine arts education. She had earned an Associate of Arts degree from Galloway Woman's College in Hendricks, Arkansas. She had continued her studies in Dallas at Cocke's School of Expression, in Chicago, and in Atlanta at the same school when Minnie Pearl studied. All her teachers told her she had a fine soprano voice and loads of talent. She didn't have a four-year degree, but it was thought sufficient for the time. When she completed her education, she went to teach speech and voice at Heavener High School in Oklahoma. There she met and married my father, a handsome young man about town.

Of course, when she married, she had to give up teaching whether she wanted to or not. Married women weren't allowed to teach. I have no idea where this rule came from. It had something to do with the depression and not paying two salaries into one family. I suppose it seemed logical to the school boards of those times.

When Mother left my father to come to Raymondville, she applied for a teaching position. She had experience. Her credentials were impeccable and certainly far superior to any other teacher's in the entire county.

Except that she was divorced. The school principal of Robert E. Lee Elementary Mrs. Adeline Pittman looked down her long thin nose. "You're wasting your time."

Mrs. Pittman, the daughter of a Methodist minister, was straight-laced beyond belief. With sanctimony worthy of the Spanish Inquisition, she saved the morals of the youth from such an unsavory female.

Mother came home with red-rimmed eyes. She and Mammaw sent me out to play in the salt cedars while they talked.

The next week, Mother went to San Perlita. It was the third largest town in the county with a small school that went to the eighth grade only. Unfortunately, Mrs. Pittman had phoned the principal there. My mother was told they didn't need any teachers. When she protested, begged probably, the woman seemed to relent slightly. Mother could have private students after school.

I never knew how she sought those students, but I know what happened when she drove to San Perlita to meet with her first class. She came home with such a look of disappointment on her face that even I recognized it. She dropped down at the kitchen table and put her head in her hand. Her cheeks were wet with tears.

"There wasn't anybody there," she said. Her voice quivered. "The school was dark. Locked up tight."

Mammaw put her hand on my mother's shoulder. She hugged her hard. I hugged her. We three held each other there in the kitchen.

We were all we had.

Then Mother dried her eyes. The phone company was the only solution. Mammaw didn't want her to go to work at all even with the family finances in a precarious state. She particularly didn't want her working in the phone company. Who knew what might happen, who she might encounter? She might be corrupted.

Telephone operators were called "Hello, Girls," because at first they said "Hello" to whoever placed a call. The consensus of opinion was that they couldn't be very "nice" because they talked to strange men albeit over a wire perhaps miles away. Who knows what else they might say? Or what the men might say to them?

But Mother swore she would be good. She went to work for ten cents an hour, nine hours a day, six days a week. When she needed to use the bathroom, she went across the alley to the supervisor's house.

She had a car, so she occasionally would take extra work delivering night letters for one dollar each. Those were telegrams or emergency phone calls that came in after the office had officially closed down. (She delivered the telegram to Ruth Mix that brought the news that her father Tom Mix, the Western movie star, had been killed in a car crash in Arizona.) In that way she made more money than anybody else at the company, more money than many people in town did including the men.

All this working and driving around convinced everyone in Raymondville that she was "not a nice girl" and "no wonder her husband divorced her." She said "hello" to strange men and drove all over the countryside at night. My mother blackened her reputation because she refused to allow her mother and daughter to starve in genteel poverty. To her way of thinking, she had no choice.

She worked as a telephone operator for twenty-nine years.

Besides destroying her reputation, the heavy headsets and bells and static eventually destroyed her hearing.

But we were never hungry or cold. And the proudest day of her life was when I received my Master's Degree qualifying me to teach in both high school and college education. She had seen to it that what happened to her would never happen to me.

ππ π

One reason I had looked forward to life on the farm was because I thought that I would have my own horse. Of course, it wouldn't be as wonderful as Dan, my uncle's mahogany bay gelding. I'd probably have a short, fat pinto pony. But I was going to live on a farm. Farms had horses.

I was bitterly disappointed. Milk cows, we had. Flocks of chickens. Litters of kittens. Pens of pigs. But no horse.

I don't think my grandmother nor my mother ever understood how I wished for a horse. Of course, I didn't realize how little my mother knew about horses. She couldn't saddle it for me or take care of it. And she couldn't run the risk that I would be injured by an animal that big. I felt bereft and betrayed as if a promise had been broken. If I had only known, I could have stayed with Gaggy and Tom—or maybe Uncle Orr himself.

But of course that was impossible. Mammaw explained to me that we were poor, too poor for animals that couldn't produce eggs, milk, and meat or keep the rats out of the barn. We couldn't buy feed for luxury animals with what we might need to buy gasoline for the tractor and the car and kerosene for the lanterns. Although we had our own water well turned by a windmill, we still had to buy propane gas for the tank to burn in the stoves. Later when we got electricity, we had to pay for it rather than kerosene.

So I never had a horse.

But Dan, my uncle's beautiful saddle mount.

In my memory.

When Gene Autry sang "Back in the Saddle Again" on the 78-Record on the windup Victrola, I sang along lustily as if I were singing to Dan. Gene's horse Champion was a fine horse, a bay as well, but Dan was undoubtedly better. After all Champion had three white stockings. All real horsemen knew that white hooves were frequently softer and more likely to split than black.

Then the letter came. Tucked in a paragraph midway down the page, Aunt Flo told my mother that Uncle Orr and Doctor Harvey had been taking their horses to a rodeo when the trailer turned over. One of the slats in the side had splintered and gone through Dan's chest. He was dead.

I don't think my mother was equipped to handle my grief. Now, more than half a century later, my heart still squeezes tight in my chest, my throat aches, and my eyes prickle. The prince of horses, the sublime mount of gods and little girls was dead. How could such an awful thing happen? There was no justice, no right. The other horse was barely scratched.

I wept copiously. I begged for the letter. I looked at the paragraph trying to read it, though at four I couldn't read the script. I took it away with me to climb up into the salt cedars where I sat forlorn.

I began to sing. "Good-bye, Old Dan, I'll see you no more."

Sobbing and singing, rocking, holding the letter, I let grief take me where it would.

My mother came out and stood under the tree with her hands on her hips. Her lips were twitching. She thought I was funny.

I hated her.

Mammaw came up behind her and told me to come down. When I did—reluctantly—she took the letter away.

Mother scolded me. Dan was only a horse.

Mammaw told me I was going to make myself sick crying.

I realized Mother wasn't taking me seriously. I was hurt all over again. How embarrassing! They doubted the sincerity of my mourning. They thought it was childish and silly.

But it wasn't!

I was angry with Mother for weeks. I overheard her telling the story of my sitting in the tree, sobbing and singing, with streaming, swollen eyes and nose and a red, unlovely face. Everyone smiled and joined in to tease me from grief.

I think I know why.

Real grief is too deep to be shared. The ugly toll of grief on the face, the voice, the routine of life is wasteful. It must be put aside, tucked away, hidden from those who cannot or will not share it. The living must take up where they left off and go on as if nothing has happened.

No one knew that something very important had happened to me. My heart was softened. When cowboys had to shoot their horses on the silver screen, I wept. When a favorite pet died, I mourned.

From the accidental death of a beloved animal, miles away, I learned to grieve, to recognize loss and what it truly meant.

More was lost with his death. An important link with my family in Oklahoma was gone with him. Things wouldn't be the same when I returned. The mahogany bay gelding with his ebony mane and tail had been part of the happiness that I'd known there.

When I went back to Oklahoma for a visit, I expected to share some of my burden with Uncle Orr, but like the other adults he'd thrown it off and passed on. He didn't act particularly sad. He had bought a new horse—buckskin.

Bucky was more expensive, a trained cutting horse, my uncle said. He took her halter and brought her up to the porch for Mother and me to admire. She had feet like a cat, he said.

I thought her pale dun skin as ugly as anything I'd ever seen. She had a white streak down her nose too. Everyone knew that white streaks and spots made the horse's skin weak.

Four white feet and a white nose.
Cut off his skin and feed him to the crows.

I couldn't stand the thought of her standing in Dan's stall or being outfitted with Dan's saddle with the leather roses pressed into the fenders.

I wasn't allowed to ride Bucky. She was too spirited. I suspect my uncle didn't want her "ruined" by my childish fumbling. Dan had been patient. He'd trusted Dan, he said. But Bucky was too high-strung. He saddled Babe—Aunt Flo's mild-tempered, undistinguished sorrel. I rode because I loved to, but it was never going to be the same.

A few months later Harley Warren, who had become one of my grandmother's best and most loyal friends, came by to say that he had made arrangements for Ruth to have a horse to ride for the afternoon. Of all the men in the Valley, he was the one Mammaw trusted and could depend on completely.

Not until now do I remember the chunky brown horse that stood patiently under a tree in Harley's front yard while Ruth petted it. It was saddled and bridled, the reins tied round the trunk.

I hurried over to join her. I rubbed my hand over its forehead, smoothed its mane, caressed its velvet muzzle. I inhaled the distinctive scent of horse and saddle leather.

Harley and Mammaw watched us from the front porch of his little house. Then he came down to help me up on the horse. I shrugged him off. I could mount it by myself.

I think I rode twice or three times more than Ruth, who really didn't care all that much about horses. I remember her saying, "How do you get him to gallop? I can't get him to gallop."

But gallop I did, with the wind in my hair and his mane whipping back in my face covering up the occasional tears because he wasn't Dan. I was like a burr on his back. No child anywhere in the world was more alive than I at that moment.

And until this moment, I never thought anything strange about that day. But now as I write these lines, I wonder. Did my grandmother instigate that healing time for me?

For all the rest of my life, I'll believe she did.

πππ

Jack Damron was one of the first people I met when Mother and I moved to the Valley. He was handsome beyond belief, deeply tanned from the sun, his black hair waving, his white teeth flashing in a glorious warm smile. He was irresistible to both men and women.

And he knew he was.

Aunt Jane and he had married two years before in 1935. Now he was farming Mammaw's quarter section with the help of our black tractor driver and man-of-all-work John.

I didn't know at that time that Jack was only nineteen years old and more of a boy than a man. I thought he was wonderful.

His real name was Clarence Allen, but that name had disappeared early in his youth. Everyone who knew him called him Jack and took to him immediately.

He could sing and play a guitar so engagingly that no one could help smiling, drawing near in delight, braving being caught in the almost gypsy glamour that radiated from his darkly handsome face and direct black gaze. When he sang "El Rancho Grande" and "The Strawberry Roan," his infectious joy would lift the listener out of himself completely.

In another life he would have cut the perfect figure, clad in motley, to lead the rats out of Hamlin.

He would have led the children too. They would have followed him gladly, unable and unwilling to forego the magic of his clever fingers making music.

Even the weather seemed unable to resist him. He'd stand on the back porch, hands on his hips, head thrown back. His Indian black eyes would stare at the horizon fiercely. "It's gonna rain," he'd sing. "It's gonna rain. I gotta feelin' it's gonna rain."

He'd grin up at the burning blue sky and the cloudless horizon and then grin down at me.

I'd look up into that blinding, electric expression, my whole being trying to discover what was real and what was fairy tale.

And then before I knew it, the clouds would begin to build in the east. A rumble would sound far off over the Gulf. The wind would come, rushing toward us. The salt cedars would bend and stream before it.

I'd see it coming. Like a silver wall. I'd leap for the porch. Sometimes, the first huge drops would splatter my bare heels.

Boiling behind them, came dark clouds bursting with water, with lightning forking and playing out before them. Thunder clapped in our ears, and huge splattering drops spilled onto the gray dust.

Somehow he'd made it happen. I loved him to distraction.

I'm sure he recognized the hero worship and he made no effort to allay it. In fact he basked in it.

Sometimes after supper while my mother and Aunt Jane were doing the dishes, he'd take a nickel from his pocket and press it hard against the skin of his upper arm. And right before my eyes it would "slip beneath his skin." He'd grin and pull his hand away and wink at Jane.

She'd smile back, happy that he'd taken the time to play with me, looking forward to the day when they'd have children of their own for him to play with.

I'd stare in pure amazement. In the skin of his arm was the imprint of the buffalo. He'd done as he'd promised—made it slip beneath the skin.

But how?

"It's not there," I'd say, shaking my head, struggling to keep my own disbelief from creeping into my voice, struggling to resist his charm. "It's not."

He'd grin and wink.

I couldn't resist him. "Take it out."

Like magic his hand would rub hard against the spot, and the nickel would come out and away on the tips of his index and third fingers.

Even though I wasn't a fool, I didn't see the sleight of hand. I didn't want to, but oh, how I believed!

One afternoon I ran to meet him when he drove in early. His smile was not quite the same, but very close. On the back porch he held out his hand for Mammaw to cut the string he'd tied so tight at the base of his third finger. The finger was blue and swollen twice its normal size. When he'd bent to pick up a Texas gate, he hadn't seen the rattler curled beneath—until it struck.

I had to hide my eyes when I saw the deep X sliced just above the knuckle. He'd cut the X himself with his pocketknife and let the rattler's poison drain away with the blood. Then he'd tied the string with the end in his teeth to be sure. And now he grinned and winked at me while Mammaw cleaned it and gave him ice water.

I thought he was magical and so brave. How could someone cut himself so deep and still smile? How could anyone not panic with rattlesnake venom headed for his heart?

Two years passed and his son, my cousin Allen Wayne Damron, was born. I was going to have a little boy to play with. I peered at the baby wrapped in a blue and white blanket cradled in his mother's arms. Allen looked back at me with Jack's black eyes from beneath soft wisps of Jack's black hair.

I swear his mouth lifted in the faintest hint of Jack's smile. I lost my heart all over again.

And then somehow for some reason I never knew, Jack was gone. And Mammaw had to find someone else to farm our land.

Aunt Jane left too. She went to Harlingen twenty miles away to work in a dress shop. I suppose she wasn't willing to face the contempt of the good people of Raymondville when she got a divorce. She wasn't willing to be a "Hello Girl" either, even if being one meant she could come home every night and hug her child, the way her sister was doing.

Both Jack and Jane, it seemed to me, climbed into their cars like gypsies and disappeared into the night. They left their son with Mammaw and Mother and with me.

All that magic, all those brilliant smiles, all that stirring music didn't take proper care of his family. The flaming red hair and beautiful face offered the explanation that she could make more money in Harlingen.

Mammaw never said anything about them leaving Allen.

Except once.

"Mammaw," I asked sassily one night, "why doesn't Allen have to eat his turnip greens? You always make me eat everything on my plate."

She reached over and touched my cheek. "Because you have a mother who loves you," she said softly. "He doesn't have either father or mother."

ππ π

Allen was reared in a house of women. Not so many women actually, but three very determined desperate females can seem like a whole battalion. Such were his "Mammaw," his "Auntie Momma" as he called my mother, and me, his "Sister."

My grandmother must have worried because he didn't have any men to pattern himself after. Just as she worked to ensure that my father's hot temper didn't dominate my life, she worked to make Allen a manly man. She wanted to give him all the advantages that we could offer him—music, literature, manners, education—while at the same time she was determined that his masculinity did not suffer.

On no account would he be allowed to become a sissy.

To that end she insisted that he do all sorts of gentlemanly things for her even when he was small. He opened doors for her; he held her chair at the table. He walked on the outside of the sidewalk. He addressed everyone older as ma'am or sir. Of course, we both did that. He was always encouraged to be daring. He didn't have a problem because he had me to lead him around.

Aunt Jane taught him to light her cigarette for her. For that reason he always carried a lighter long before he smoked.

The older he grew, the more we adored him because he treated us exactly the way we'd taught him to. We created the perfect gentleman, the man who respected and admired women and treated them well. He never lost his court-ly manners, never failed to speak of and treat women with utmost courtesy. Women fell in love with him within minutes because as the years passed he became more and more a rarity—a perfect gentleman.

Mammaw further believed in a good education. I was enlisted to read my lessons to him every night. He was taught piano and dance as well. His education included the arts.

I was educated too. When I became a schoolteacher, I could read for hours using expression and sometimes acting out exciting parts of the texts for the benefit of my students. I'm sure Mammaw never had that in mind when she put me to work, but I'm so glad she did.

Allen had inherited his father's talent in music. He had perfect pitch and a wonderful singing voice. He made his living for years as an entertainer in both concert and club.

But all those things weren't manly pursuits. Mammaw knew fishing, but Willacy County had no rivers or even creeks. It had bar ditches and canals where careless children frequently drowned, but they were shallow with not many fish of a good size.

She decided that Allen, because he was a boy, must learn to swim. If I learned too, that was all right, but he was the priority. Nobody had a swim-ming pool in his backyard. In fact in all of Raymondville, there wasn't one except at the country club. Of course, we couldn't afford to belong, but we had Red Fish Bay and El Sal Viejo only a few miles from our door.

Unfortunately, Mammaw couldn't swim. In fact, she was deathly afraid of water. So careful was she to conceal her fear, that neither Allen nor I ever suspected. We jumped right in while she held her breath and clenched her fists so tight her fingernails made red moons on her palms.

As a backup, Mammaw again enlisted the aid of her good friends the Warrens. Several times, Mammaw and Harley and his wife Lillian took their daughter Ruth and Allen and me to the seashore of the Gulf of Mexico and the lakeshore of the old salt lake. Since none of the adults could swim and there were no lifeguards, how did they dare?

Mammaw devised a simple but foolproof scheme. She tied one end of a clothesline rope around each of our waists and tied the other end to the bumper of the Chevrolet.

That day we'd moved from department to department for nearly half an hour. Mother had scanned the racks, looking at some dresses intently, memorizing the waists and skirts and trim. She'd turned hats around and around and tried them on until I was stomping and whining with boredom.

She was holding a piece of material by the corner, feeling the quality of the goods and thinking how well it would launder when a saleslady approached. "May I help you?"

Mother started to speak, but I was quicker. I already knew the answer. "No," I said righteously. "We don't have any money. We're just looking."

The saleslady looked from me to the edge of the piece of material Mother was holding. Mother dropped it, grabbed my hand, and practically ran out of the store.

Mother told several people what I'd done and how embarrassed she'd been. She actually told Aunt Jane she was considering buying that piece of material, but I'd ruined it for her. She recited the poem to me and explained for the umpteenth time what it meant.

I was upset and resentful. Why did she have to tell everyone what I'd done? She'd told me herself that we couldn't buy anything. If we were going to buy something, why did she tell me a story? And then I figured it out. She didn't want me to beg for anything in that expensive store.

I was proud of myself for being smart enough to figure her reason out, but for years I wondered at the subtleties of my mother's mind. When would I be smart enough to see into the double meaning of people's words? When would I be able to understand what people *really* meant?

I couldn't! Not for years. I was a little pitcher with big ears and a lightning mouth. I heard everything and told all I knew. The most embarrassing event in my mother's adventures in childrearing occurred as a result of her trying to correct my grammar.

Actually, as I look back on it, I consider it a sort of revenge—a very small measure of revenge—not a very nice revenge—but then revenge is never nice. Although it occurred before the deed that called for vengeance, I've never forgotten it.

Grandmother and Grandfather Young both said "ain't." They had never finished high school, but married as teenagers and come from farms in South Carolina to work on the Kansas City Southern Railroad.

The year we lived with them when I was two-going-on-three, my mother was between a rock and a hard place. She couldn't correct me in front of them without hurting their feelings and making them think she looked down on them. On the other hand, she herself never said "ain't" and didn't intend that her daughter should sound like some illiterate clodhopper.

When she tried to explain things to me discreetly, I refused to be explained to. If my Gaggy and Granddad Tom said "ain't," I was going to say "ain't." I was obdurate about it.

"I ain't going to quit it," I said and thrust out my lower lip.

Mother was irritated beyond belief. I was secretly pleased. It was my way to get her goat.

Sometimes I'd make sentences that didn't make sense, so I could use the word "ain't" to make my mother angry. I was the very devil, tormenting her.

One day after we'd lived in the Valley for several months, an invitation came in the mail for my grandmother. At that time the "good" people in the Valley had, for the most part, forgotten the Widow Bevens sitting out on her dirt farm. A number of men were casting speculative eyes at the quarter section of fertile land wondering what it would take to get it for themselves.

Mammaw was invited to take tea at Sister Jaco's. She wanted very much to go and perhaps enlist the good woman's support especially since the invitation included my mother. The "nice" ladies of Raymondville hadn't received Mother since she went to work for the telephone office.

Our hostess was a frail, white-haired old lady, the wife of the Methodist Minister Emeritus of the First Methodist Church South in Raymondville. She was one of the arbiters of morality and decency in the community. She was also the mother of Mrs. Adeline Pittman, who had kept Mother from teaching school. To this day I wish Mrs. Pittman had been there.

Sister Jaco served my grandmother and mother tea in thin china cups and saucers. She served me little sugar cookies on a china plate and a little glass of lemonade.

My mother kept her eye on me all the time. She held her breath as I drank without spilling a drop and ate the cookies without scattering crumbs too badly. She watched me as I wiped my mouth on the napkin.

Sensing my mother's nervousness, Sister Jaco smiled warmly. "There's a sweet little girl. She ain't gonna hurt a thing."

I flashed my mother a look of unholy glee.

My mother's face reflected her horror. She knew what was coming. She couldn't shush me in time.

"See, Mother," I said triumphantly. "She said 'ain't.'"

Mother reported later that she was absolutely mortified. Her face turned bright red.

Mammaw put her own teacup down so quickly that the tea splashed into the saucer. She looked at me with such a look of disappointment that I cringed.

But Sister Jaco was very gracious. She understood perfectly. She leaned forward, that dear, white-haired lady, and patted me.

"That's because my mother didn't teach me any difference," she said.

Suddenly, I felt very sad as well as much embarrassed and very much ashamed. She hadn't had a mother to teach her the difference.

I could feel my own face crumpling. A lump swelled in my throat. I hung my head. Mammaw cleared her throat and began to talk about the muscadine jelly that her sister-in-law Aunt Ora had sent her from Arkansas.

I sat silent and still for the rest of the time. I learned Sister Jaco's lesson well that day. I had a mother who cared to teach me to be correct.

I broke myself of saying "ain't."

ππ π

I've always been in favor of equal rights for women. When I was only five years old, I would have marched and burned my bra and stormed the halls of Congress if anyone had asked me to. I would have done anything to get men to recognize women as equals and human beings worthy of respect. Why was I so passionate about these rights at such an early age? I saw how men treated my mother and grandmother after my grandfather's death

Suddenly, common decency and the brotherhood of man were only for the brothers. Men who would have helped my grandfather without a second thought, men who claimed to be his wife's friend as well as his, disdained my grandmother.

Men who were my grandfather's best friends gathered like ravenous wolves when he died. They wanted the land he'd bought.

The quarter section where we lived was cleared except for the two lagoons. The half section was largely undeveloped. But it was some of the best land in the delta. It should have been relatively easy for Mammaw to hire someone— one of Pawpaw's friends—to farm it for two-thirds net share of the crops.

Two-thirds would have made the farmer well-to-do if not wealthy by the standards of the 30s and 40s. When all the bills were settled, they could have paid my grandmother the other third and we could have lived comfortably. The rich soil would grow two or even three crops a year.

But the greedy thieves wanted it all. They aligned themselves against her, warning off anyone who might have gone to work for her. They weren't willing to pay her one-third earnings for the use of prime land. Why pay her when they could sit back, refuse to work for her, and watch her lose it for taxes and for non-development? Then they could step in and buy it cheaply.

I wonder how they eased their consciences as they attended the Methodist Church that preached caring for widows and orphans. Did they tell each other that she would only have lost it anyway? Did they shrug and rationalize that they were probably saving her a lot of headaches? Did they justify their greed by saying that women didn't know anything about farming? Did they think of themselves as smart businessmen?

Did Aunt Jane marry Jack Damron to save the land? I wonder if Arch Damron, his father, steered Jack into he marriage to get the land indirectly. Jack was seventeen; Jane was twenty. They certainly didn't love each other very much.

All of 1936 Mammaw tried to find someone to farm for her. Then with some reservations she turned it over to her young son-in-law, who put in a crop.

The first year after the cotton was harvested, Jack didn't pay Mammaw all she was entitled to. Indeed, he gave her barely enough to pay the taxes. Perhaps he treated his mother-in-law and his wife the way Arch Damron treated his wife Verda. Perhaps he thought that Mammaw and Aunt Jane wouldn't know what to do with the money. Perhaps he thought they'd just waste it. Perhaps he reasoned that they grew their food to eat and they had plenty of clothes.

Perhaps he was greedy.

Mammaw finally demanded the rest of the money. She found she couldn't get it. He claimed he already spent it—partly on fram improvements.

When my mother and I arrived, she immediately set to work to remedy the situation. She was frustrated at every turn.

She soon realized that with her divorced status, no one respected her. She got a host of offers, but none to farm her mother's land. Men would smile at her, squeeze her shoulder, and hug her too tightly. At this point she probably would have been willing to marry one of them, but no one offered to marry her. Everybody knew Mrs. Bevens would get tired and sell out in a few months. No sense taking on a passel of women.

The second year, Mother took Mammaw directly to the gins and packing sheds. My grandmother asked the owners and operators to pay the crop checks directly to her. They said they couldn't do that.

"Jack Damron's your farmer," they said. They didn't even say they were sorry.

Then she demanded that they cut two checks, two-thirds for Jack and one-third for her. They refused. Did they hide malicious grins behind their hands? If she'd let that fool boy farm her land, she deserved to lose it.

Of course, they told Jack that his mother and sister-in-law had been to see them. He and Aunt Jane had a terrible argument. It ended with his working himself into a rage, getting into his car and driving off in a cloud of dust. Aunt Jane came crying to Mammaw, who was sorry that she had to upset her daughter's family, but she stood firm. She had to have her money—or a new farmer.

Meanwhile, Mother ran the wheels off the car trying to find someone. Just when it seemed no one could save the widow's farm, Glenn Bailey appeared.

He was a young man without a place. His wife Goldie was the daughter of a man who'd been about to help Pawpaw clear the big undeveloped acreage. Glenn and Goldie were young and energetic. Their daughter Marlene was just a year older than I.

Glenn had nothing to lose and everything to gain. He wouldn't have had a chance of buying the land if Mammaw put it up for sale or lost it for taxes. If he could make a good crop and save the farm, perhaps she'd let him work the land for several more years. He saw his chance and was brave enough to take it. Mammaw contracted with him to put in the new crop.

Jack came back too late. Instead of chastened women begging to be saved, as the prodigal son-in-law, he received a cold welcome. It wasn't what he had expected, and he didn't like it one bit. Immediately, he hied himself over to give Glenn the word.

Goldie told us what he said.

"You won't like working for them. Women don't understand men's business. Jane and I are just having some trouble right now. We'll get back together and you'll be out."

"That could be," Glenn agreed.

"They don't know about farming," Jack kept on. "They want more money than they're strictly entitled to. They want it all at once. They don't understand that you've got to keep some back for emergencies."

Glenn said nothing.

Jack played his last card. "If you go to work here, you may not have a chance to work in the Valley again."

"But at least I'll work this year," Glenn said.

And work he did. He made a good crop. He paid Mammaw everything she was due right on time.

The next year Mammaw didn't think twice about whether to offer him a contract. He and his family became a fixture in the third house at the end of the lane. He farmed our land as long as Mammaw lived. After her death there was not question of his leaving. He could have a place until he retired.

Unfortunately, Glenn didn't have the heavy equipment nor the resources to hire help to clear the 635-acre section. The men in the country government cut a road through it, raised Mammaw's taxes to pay for it, and took it when she couldn't pay them.

But she was able to save the rest. It sheltered Allen and me and my mother. It fed us and earned us a living. It helped indirectly to pay for my education.

It has never for an instant been for sale.

VI
FAMILY PLEASURES

Blessed assurance. Jesus is mine.
Oh, what a foretaste of glory divine.

Across more than half a century come the voices of my grandmother, my cousin Allen, and me raised in song. On Sunday morning, on Wednesday evening, on any night or day when we had the time, or even when we didn't, we'd gather to sing. Mammaw would take us into the living room with its huge black player piano.

Although we had dozens of piano rolls, she hardly ever attached one. Mammaw played the instrument beautifully. I'm sure she could play every hymn in the hymnal because she'd played for the men's Sunday school class in the Booneville Methodist Church.

I come to the garden alone
While the dew is still on the roses,

Allen would climb up on the bench on Mammaw's left and I'd stand on her right and we'd sing. Could we carry a tune? Who cared? We sang with our hearts.

Jesus loves me. This I know,
For the Bible tells me so.

At the end of each song, Mammaw would run arpeggios up the keyboard. What a wonderful trick! I used to stare in awe, trying to figure out how to do them myself someday because those notes weren't written in the hymnal. They were made-up notes that she added all by herself. Triumphant embellishments to God's glory and the glory of music.

It was all so wonderful and so simple. Just the three of us singing and swaying, absorbing rhythm, melody, harmony, learning another language to express emotion. Allen and I didn't even know we were learning. We thought we were playing. But in those treasured hours we learned to sing.

Allen went on to become a professional singer. Fifteen years later at Lon Morris College, "Los Bandidos" brought the house down at a Lion's Club meeting.

In 1814 we took a little trip
With Colonel Andy Jackson
Down the mighty Mississipp.

From there he went to the Newport and Kerrville Folk Festivals and onward until he became a real "Texas Legend."

Michael, row the boat ashore.
Alleluia.

I went on throughout my teaching career to amaze, shock, and embarrass my high school classes by suddenly bursting into song:

Got a mule. Her name is Sal.
Fifteen miles on the Erie Canal.

Classes of American Literature were pretty sure I was crazy. Although folk songs appeared in their texts in the first six weeks, none of their previous teachers had ever actually tried to sing them. I was one crazy lady, for sure.

By the time the next year rolled around, the English Literature students had heard all about me and could relax a little and take with good will:

Where hae ye been, Lord Randal, my son?
and
Hangman, hangman, slack your rope,
Slack it for awhile--

Mammaw had been a Sunday school teacher almost from the time she was big enough to toddle around to take care of the babies. She had married the grandson and son of Methodist deacons and the brother of a Methodist minister. Since they were all gone, our religious schooling was a duty she could not forego. She took what she considered to be her obligations very seriously.

By example, she would show us good behavior. But in her own way. She would never presume to preach. By music she would show us God. She would never presume to describe Him in words.

I didn't think about why we didn't go to Sunday school, nor church, nor prayer meeting, nor choir practice. We lived in the country seven miles out of town. We had an old Chevrolet sedan. Mother took it to work six days a week.

Her excuse was that when Sunday rolled around, she was too tired to go after working all week. Perhaps she really was too tired. Or perhaps she'd become a different person—cynical and disappointed in life.

Only Mammaw never changed. She saw her duty and she did it. She filled our hearts with her favorite part of religion—the hymns, the paeans, the musical praises of God.

Sometimes the living room was hot from being closed off for the afternoon. We'd open the front door and send our salutes to the salt cedars and the road beyond. Sometimes it was cold. Mammaw would light a small gas heater with asbestos backing on the firewall, and we'd warm ourselves while we sang.

How long did we sing? I don't have any idea? Was it minutes? An hour? I can't tell.

But it put music in my soul.

πππ

When Mammaw wasn't playing hymns on the piano for us to sing, we could play ourselves—as soon as I was tall enough. Of course, the songs on the piano roles weren't hymns; but, confidentially, they were much more fun.

Actually, I can't remember when I wasn't tall enough to do most things. Mammaw had me scrambling up on chairs to reach the high shelves in the kitchen when I was four. I could do it easily.

All my height was in my legs. I was like a newborn colt that could climb to its feet and nurse within hours of its birth. I stood in my crib within months. I let go and walked at eight and a half. I ran everywhere on my tiptoes at nine. The doctor told my mother to discourage me. She rolled her eyes and suggested that he come over to show her how. He just shrugged.

The piano in our living room was a player—a magnificent black oak upright with eighty-eight lead pipes leading to the keys. Its pedals were brass, its fittings too. It probably weighed as much as a baby grand. To go with it, we had dozens of piano rolls, the early twentieth century equivalent of the CD, including one recorded by the famous concert pianist Ignace Jan Paderewski himself of his enormously popular "Menuet."

Of course, Allen and I only played the "Menuet" once. It didn't have any clever words to sing. And singing was what we wanted to do. The songs were all composed years before we were born, but their age didn't make any difference. They were all new to us.

Many of them were music hall tunes—sad songs of love. A couple of times, we played "She's Only a Bird in a Gilded Cage" because the title sounded interesting, but the tune was slow and draggy. It wasn't really about a bird.

On a really deluxe player piano like this one, the speed and the volume could be adjusted by levers behind a long box in front of and below the keyboard. We never bothered with that. We just set the speed on moderate and the volume as loud as it would go.

We sang a medley of patriotic songs including "Yankee Doodle," "When Johnny Comes Marching Home Again," and "Columbia, the Gem of the Ocean." Allen liked the bass on those. They were on his end of the piano.

Our favorite song, however, and one that we played until we wore the roll out, was "Yes, We Have No Bananas." It was a sure-fire winner guaranteed to send us off into gales of delighted laughter.

No two children could have had more fun than Allen and I when we shared that piano bench. My long skinny legs pumped wildly setting my whole body swaying. He swayed too and swung his short chubby legs.

"'We've string beans,'" I'd sing.

"' ...and scallions,'" he'd sing even though neither one of us knew what a scallion was.

"'...and cabbages.

"'...onions.'" Here we'd look at each other and grin.

Then we'd sing together. "'And all kinds of fruit and SA-A-AY!'"

His turn.

"'We have some old fashioned horse-radish.'"

I'd sing the next line. I always gave myself all the good lines. "'It's just turning baddish.'"

"'BUT YES!'" We'd always yell that. "'We have no bananas. We have no bananas toda-a-ay.'"

Sometimes I'd be pumping so hard we'd have to grab for the edge of the piano to keep from tipping the stool over with our glee.

We played "Bananas" so often the roll began to give out.

Mammaw fixed it several times, but its hook finally ripped off completely. We had to fold and hook the paper through a hole punched in the end of it. Then that made the whole roll slightly crooked, so the edges frayed. Likewise, the role now played a musical step higher and struck wrong notes occasionally.

Of course, we didn't know or care. We were having too much fun.

I'm sure we damaged the piano in some ways. Where our sweaty, grimy little legs rubbed against the bench, the varnish wore off and the veneer cracked.

When I think about that today, the damage bothers me. The piano had been one of the first gifts Mammaw received from Pawpaw. Perhaps it was her wedding gift. It certainly shows how much she loved music and how much Pawpaw loved her.

She told about a huge man who must have weighed three hundred pounds pulling up in a truck to deliver it all the way from Little Rock. She marveled how he brought it up the porch steps and into the house by himself. The player was a source of great joy to her, and I'm sure a treasured reminder of the past.

Perhaps a selfish or even a prideful woman would have kept it like a shrine with a silken shawl draped over it and her husband's picture in a silver frame on top. Certainly, she would have kept us little heathens from romping on it. What a grave mistake that would have been!

No piece of furniture in our house was better loved, or put to better use. I'm sure she thought the damage a small price to pay for the love it created. Not to speak of the talent it engendered.

πππ

My grandmother was many wonderful things.

First, she was an extraordinary caretaker of children. No one could have had a better upbringing than I did. She was a musician and an artist with silk and cotton threads. She was an endlessly creative playmate for two children without fathers and with mostly absent mothers. Because of her, we didn't even know we were lonely and deprived.

But she wasn't perfect. I must confess now, and I don't think she would dispute me.

She was a careless housekeeper—and an awful cook.

Not for me happy memories of deep dish apple pie, superb roasts, home-made jams and jellies, and fresh-baked bread. My grandmother had cooked for many years for my grandfather who couldn't eat sugar because of his diabetes, nor salt because of his high blood pressure.

So long as he lived, my grandfather preferred to do most of the cooking himself. Being the oldest child, he had cooked all the family meals in the Bevens household because his mother was ill a great deal of the time. His biscuits were rumored to float off the plate. His piecrusts were a delight. His fried chicken with cream gravy was legendary.

He was one lucky man because his wife couldn't season worth a dime. She came by her lack of skill honestly. Before she married Pawpaw, Mammaw had never had a cooking lesson. Her mother had hurriedly prepared all the family food, what little there was. Fair-Eleanor had been too busy working in the bank to serve anything but plain fare.

Mammaw's tastes were strange. She craved sugar because she'd been deprived of it for so long. Consequently, she sugared everything including vegetables. Herbs and spices were largely ignored. She hated pepper.

She knew nothing about salads. The Booneville grocery store had probably not stocked such a thing as a head of lettuce. Homemakers could make coleslaw from grated cabbage and carrots. "Salats" were edible plants from the Arkansas hills—sour dock, poke, dandelion stems, and lamb's quarters—all gathered in the spring, washed, and picked over. I've tasted all those things, and I am here to testify that "edible" does not necessarily mean "tasty."

When Mammaw did learn to make salads after we moved into town and mostly because Mother insisted, she chopped iceberg lettuce and tomatoes tossed with Miracle Whip Salad Dressing. When we grew cucumbers, Mammaw and Mother made pickles out of most of them to preserve them. Occasionally, Mammaw would slice a fresh one, put it in a dish of salted vinegar diluted by melting ice cubes. I liked it, but Allen wouldn't touch it.

Mammaw's only soup was vegetable made by opening a can of tomatoes and adding leftovers. Her sidedish vegetables were cooked the way old-timey cookbooks recommended. That is, they were boiled, mashed, buttered, and sugared and salted till all natural flavor and most nutrients were gone.

Her meat was chicken, floured, dipped in egg, floured again, and fried in lard or bacon grease. Sometimes we'd have chicken livers or calf liver prepared the same way. Mammaw did not like beef. She'd never seen a leg of lamb. She'd never cooked any shrimp or oysters that were plentiful and cheap from the Gulf.

I never saw her bake a piecrust. Cobblers were quicker. When Betty Crocker produced her first cake mix, Mammaw was there to buy it. It solved so many problems.

Of course, I wasn't critical until I got away from home and tasted foods cooked by others. Allen, on the other hand, was a picky eater. He didn't like anything.

Perhaps her cooking wouldn't have been so bad if we hadn't been living eight hundred miles south of all the ingredients she'd learned to use.

In those days the selection of foodstuffs varied and consequently the cookery in Central Arkansas was different from the tip of South Texas. Foods that Mammaw was used to preparing fresh had to be canned or dried to be shipped. Local farmers and dairymen brought their fresh produce into Raymondville in the backs of pickup trucks and sold it direct to Brenner's Grocery, the couple of cafes, the boarding houses, and the Ramon Hotel. What was left was sold in the open market and door to door.

Brenner's was a small grocery store. Its meat market was in the back. Since this was the coolest part of the store, the fresh vegetable bins were back there too. The selection consisted of green peppers, yellow summer squash, acorn winter squash, Idaho potatoes. Some shelves for canned and packaged stuff made aisles and covered the other walls.

Frozen food was non-existent. In fact most homes had only iceboxes to which the iceman delivered blocks of ice. Fresh foodstuffs could be shipped only at considerable expense around the country in refrigerator cars on the railroads. The vegetables were put in the refrigerator cars and covered with ice that melted and had to be replaced frequently. Of course, delicate spring vegetables and summer fruits and berries couldn't be shipped.

My grandmother's best dishes were the ones she herself liked to eat— fried chicken, mashed potatoes with cream gravy made from the grease used to fry the chicken, and a No. 2 can of English peas. In season we had sliced tomatoes and squash. Our main meals were pretty much the same thing with oatmeal or scrambled eggs for breakfast and bacon sandwiches or soup for supper.

I never minded. If Mammaw set it on the table, it tasted good to me. What did I know? I ate it down in great bites and dashed out to swing and play in the salt cedars, to run the calories off in a couple of hours and come back for more.

Sometimes when I came back in, Allen and I received a treat that even he couldn't pick at—banana rolls. They were the one treat Mammaw could prepare better than anyone else in the whole world—or so we believed—while Allen and I milled around her getting in the way as hard as we tried to help.

Mammaw would roll out a recipe of Bisquick on a floured tabletop, the pantry door that swung its single leg down into the center of the kitchen. Meanwhile, the lard was heating in the deep skillet. She would cut the thinly rolled dough into four-inch squares. She'd place an eighth of a big banana on the diagonal across each square. She'd sprinkle it with sugar and cinnamon. She'd add a dab of butter.

She didn't trust oleomargarine. Anything that was white as lard and had a capsule of red food coloring to be mashed up in it was surely dangerous.

She'd roll the ingredients up and seal the ends. Then she'd drop four or six of them at a time into the hot fat.

They'd sizzle as she rolled them with the spatula so they'd cook evenly. In a minute or two they'd turn golden brown, and out they'd come. She'd put them on a paper napkin to drain. Then she'd move them to a plate where she'd sprinkled them with more sugar.

Most times the three of us would eat the whole batch. The cinnamon and sugar, the nearly melted banana, the hot melted butter would run into our mouths on the first bite.

The gods should have had such nectar. We were pagans, the three of us, gorging ourselves with Olympian gusto on the very best that the world has to offer. Hot delicious food served and shared with love.

The preparing, serving, and sharing of a dish is an act of communion. In this case it was a communion of joy. Our ages—three, seven, and fifty-five disappeared. By it we were united forever.

π π π

Over the years I've loved to joke and say that I was reared in the Rio Theatre in Raymondville. For nine cents and a nickel's worth of popcorn, a huge greasy sack of the stuff, I could spend the Saturday afternoon alone with two feature Westerns, a cartoon, a travelogue, a serial, and the Movietone News.

Mammaw and Mother could get all their shopping done for the week and probably get a respite from me—their wild child. What they did without me bouncing and whining and twisting on the end of their arms, I didn't know. Or care. I never suspected I was being babysat. I thought I was incredibly lucky.

Of course, the Westerns were the only movies I ever saw. I drank in the heroism, the moral behavior, the clean-cut good looks of Gene Autry with his sidekick Frog Millhouse, Roy Rogers with Gabby Hayes, the Durango Kid with Fuzzy Knight, Hoot Gibson, Colonel Tim McCoy, Bob Steele, Ken Maynard, Johnny Mack Brown, Hopalong Cassidy, the Lone Ranger and Tonto, and on and on. I confess I didn't have a favorite. I loved them all.

Before little boys and little girls idolized sports stars, they idolized Western heroes. These handsome, steely-eyed men appeared every Saturday afternoon in wonderfully entertaining morality plays that helped to shape a generation now old and bewildered.

The cowboy heroes were pure as Knights Templar of old. In fact, they might kiss the girl, but only if they blocked the prurient sight behind their ten-gallon hats. They blushed and stammered when the girl smiled shyly at them.

Their actions were never in question. They were the epitome of Davy Crockett's motto: "Be sure you're right. Then go ahead."

If the land were in jeopardy, it must be preserved for the people, in most cases the girl, to whom it belonged. Likewise, the only things worth fighting for were land and honor.

Later, cowboys sought revenge for evil done to them, but their natural goodness kept them from doing evil even then. Memories of their mothers and their sisters called them back from the edge. Silent and stern, they sat on their magnificent horses and administered justice against the backdrop of the Chowchilla Ranch in southern California. Later when movies became more sophisticated and more expensive, they moved to Monument Valley, the High Sierras, the Redwood Forest, or the Staked Plains.

The villain, dressed all in black, was not so horrible that the hero should do something bad for vengeance. Audiences knew his own evil nature would bring about his ultimate punishment, and he would likely perish miserably by the fate he had intended for the hero.

The cowboys were unfailingly kind to their animals—an important lesson for all children. Horses were particularly treasured because they were the cowboy's partner. Everyone believed that Trigger, Champion, and Silver had been around their riders so long that they were almost as smart Roy, Gene, and the Lone Ranger. I suspect now that the tricks the horses could perform, like counting with their hooves or galloping to cowboy's rescue were taught them by their trainers for the express purpose of giving them the appearance of extraordinary intelligence. They were part and parcel of the whole heroic package.

The cowboys were clean. How this cleanliness was achieved, I never knew. Doubtless by private ablutions that included shaves, haircuts, well-pressed clothes, polished boots. My stints in the horse-barn at my uncle's and my real life chores among the chickens, pigs, and cows made me marvel at their condition—but never question. I knew a farm was a messy place. Ranches were acres and acres of waving grasslands.

One of the jobs kind cowboys often did was drag a tiny white-faced calf out of a mud-hole and carry it home across the saddlebow. Wonder of wonders, the muddy calf didn't get the cowboy dirty, but I never thought about that discrepancy.

Like Galahad's white armor, their shirts were never soiled—nor did the tails come out of their pants even after barroom brawls occasioned by some reprehensible and unshaven barfly or villain's henchman.

In the saloon Ken Maynard invariably ordered sarsaparilla, while his partner Hoot Gibson—Mammaw's favorite cowboy—would confound the bartender by ordering milk. The other cowboys would make fun of them for ordering sissy drinks, but they stood firm. They refused to do what they knew wasn't right—that is, drink any liquid that contained alcohol.

The only person who used tobacco anywhere on the screen was the leader of the villainous gang. He always wore a black business suit and on occasion he brandished an unlit cigar. I think I saw a villain blow smoke in Hopalong Cassidy's face on one or two occasions, but that act branded him as irretrievably rude as well as villainous.

All these simple lessons were repeated over and over in movies with heroic names like *Westward Bound, Lone Star Trail,* and *Marshal of Gunsmoke.* Did I just naturally figure all this proper behavior for myself? I doubt that I did. I don't think I was that perceptive. I wouldn't even have thought about the morals of the tales for myself.

My grandmother pointed them out to me while she ironed or shelled peas or crocheted. She was bothered by the sight of cowboys shot off saloon roofs, off the backs of horses, or down in the street after a quick-draw face-off.

She told me I mustn't look at shooting and killing as proper behavior. Our world was civilized. The cowboys had made it that way with their stands against outlaws and landgrabbers. Today, thanks to the cowboys, we have policemen and courts and laws. They had to use extreme measures for justice to protect good people.

And we must be good. No one expected us to be perfect. But we must be honest and kind, polite and clean. We mustn't drink or smoke.

The cowboys taught me well because to this day, I can't think of a better way to behave.

Even now, when I sit in a movie theatre and see a monstrous man, naked to the waist, bathed in sweat and besmeared with grime, shooting a whole row of equally ugly, violent men, I confess I don't see the point.

When the noise of screams, crashes, and explosions makes me cover my ears, I long to return to the thrilling days of yesteryear. Perhaps the enemies are more vicious now. Certainly the weapons are more deadly, but is the danger really any greater? Could we really not be saved by a tall, raw-boned, broad-shouldered figure on a fiery horse with the speed of light? In my heart I'm confident that he would survey the situation with keen-eyed appraisal after which a single silver bullet would bring justice for all.

πππ

I took my first dancing class at four years of age. My mother had to drive twenty-seven miles each way for me to study tap, acrobatics, and ballet from Markoleta Greer Elstner. Mother didn't have aspirations for me to grow up to be Anna Pavlova or Ruth St. Denis, whom Mother had seen dance on the stage in Chicago. I wasn't going to be Ginger Rogers either. I'd never even heard of much less seen any of those people.

What the lessons were supposed to do was "make me graceful."

That was the civilized phrase for helping me to coordinate my gangly body with its long legs and arms. No dance teacher would have accepted the task had she but known. Just a glance at me would have invalidated the contract.

I was what was politely known as "big for my age."

Farm food, fresh air, challenging exercise, and good genes had created a four-year-old who looked like six. I even talked more or less like an adult because neither Mammaw nor Mother believed in baby talk. They had talked to me in more or less adult language since the hour of my birth.

I believe Mammaw was the instigator of the dancing lessons. She loved dancing even though she'd never danced a step in her life. The Methodist Church would have been scandalized if Mrs. O. M. Bevens had ever even skipped or turned too quickly. Not that she wouldn't have loved to, I'm sure. She kept me supplied with enough half circle and full circle skirts to swirl and twirl in.

Strong instincts for grace and beauty must have been inherent in her. She couldn't have had visions of my swirling those skirts and tapping like Eleanor Powell or Ginger Rogers. At that time she'd never even gone to see a movie. Perhaps she knew that a new time was coming for my generation, and she wanted me to be inspired by graceful clothes to be graceful.

I must have been a sight in the dance studio. Long, long arms and legs that looked even longer because of the slender bones with big feet and hands flopping at the end of them.

When Mrs. Elstner first caught sight of me, she looked quickly away. I suspect she closed her eyes. She might have suppressed a snigger. Perhaps she prayed for inner strength. Then she looked back at my mother and let her hand drift to my head. I still wonder what she truly thought.

She had danced professionally in New York, but her dancing days must have been many, many years behind her. Her hair was iron gray and she was very heavy. She herself did not dance any more. She had an assistant Miss Jack, who demonstrated the steps.

Tap was probably what I was best suited for. I learned basic time steps and weight changes without too much trouble. From swinging through the salt cedars, I had a good sense balance, and my muscles were well developed from all that climbing.

Mammaw had developed my senses of rhythm and musicality by playing the piano and teaching me to sing. Mother also encouraged me to sing along with her whenever we drove anywhere in the car. As I think back about tap, I might have been pretty good at it.

As for ballet, although my turnout was lamentable, I could control my body *en balance* and do a fairly good job with simple *pas de bourrées, pas de chats,* and *glissades.*

What I could not do was acrobatics. Here I was not only graceless. I was simply unable.

My long body growing at a terrific rate had very tight tendons and muscles. Even my skin was tight. At one point I actually developed silver stretch marks on the outsides of my thighs. At night my whole body ached and jerked from growing pains. Mammaw complained about sleeping with me because I "galloped all night long."

Most girls in the class could bend over to put their palms flat on the floor without bending their knees. I couldn't even touch my toes. It seemed to me that they were too far away. I couldn't do backbends or bridge-ups. My spine simply wouldn't curve sufficiently. Front-overs and back-overs were suicide attempts. And, of course, I couldn't do the splits.

But I attempted everything with good will. And I practiced diligently at home frequently crashing to the floor and taking some inoffensive piece of furniture with me.

Mammaw encouraged me in all this. It was supposed to make me graceful. It was supposed to help me make good use of my body. Ever so often, I'd check my body in front of the mirror. Was it more graceful?

I'd strike a pose and then work on it. Could I get the arch in my foot to look like Miss Jack's? Could I open my fingers and curve them like a ballerina? Could I arch my upper back and turn my body *croisé*? Could I open it *á longé*?

Even at four my brain knew and treasured all those beautiful French words. My body just couldn't translate them.

Those dance lessons were the beginning of a long love/hate affair with my body. I have studied ballet for years and still continue to stretch and balance and turn. I still try to make myself graceful.

As with so much else in my life, my grandmother and mother set a goal for me to strive for—one they never really expected me to attain. The striving was the achievement.

$$\pi \pi \pi$$

At the same time my grandmother gave me dance lessons, she started physical education at home. She believed in constantly challenging me with both physical and mental activities. Looking back, I realize I was the luckiest child in the world. What a shame that her father didn't let her go off to college! What an educator she would have made!

At Mammaw's direction John made me a pair of stilts—not the easy little-kid kind with three-foot-long one-by-two's and little steps six inches off the ground. These were not play stilts. These were real. These were the kind of stilts that farmers in long times past might use to wade through duck-ponds and peat bogs. The Valley didn't have such things, but Mammaw must have seen then and known how to instruct John to them.

If a toy manufacturer were to market these today, they would be in the categories with skateboards and skis. Furthermore, they'd come with a disclaimer that parents couldn't sue the company when the child broke his arm.

At Mammaw's direction John cut the boards five feet long, quite a bit above my head. For the steps, she had him saw an eighteen-inch piece of two-by-four diagonally and brad those pieces on to the one by two's so that the place to put my feet was four inches wide, but the bottom of the stilts were still one by two. Then he nailed straps to the platforms to keep my feet from sliding off.

Did I have sense enough to be afraid? Of course not. The minute I saw them I wanted to walk on them. In fact, I couldn't wait too.

Let me say at the beginning, that no one can teach anyone how to walk stilts, anymore than someone can hold someone else's hand while he's trying to learn to skateboard. Any grip from any side just throws the walker or skater off balance.

I started by leaning the stilts against the side of the house and stepping between them. I put first one foot and then the other onto the steps and hoisted myself up. My back was braced against the wall. I wrapped my hands around them—and pushed off.

The first time I merely rocked forward and bumped back again. Mammaw and John were both watching me with encouraging smiles.

The next push off, I pushed too far and simply fell over.

Fortunately, I was agile as a monkey. I leaped out of the stilts when I felt myself about to go. Mammaw must have been counting on that.

I tried again. This time I balanced erect for a few seconds before I tilted back against the wall. I glanced in their direction. They nodded and smiled. Then John went off about his business and Mammaw went in the house.

I tried again. And again. If I pushed too hard, I'd have to take one staggering step and then fall headlong. But I was controlling the stilts even as I fell. They were no longer toppling helter-skelter to either side or crossing over each other and scuffing my legs and ankles. Moreover, I had got the hang of the leap. I didn't think a thing about it. I knew just how to land, just how much to bend my knees and ankles to avoid shock.

At last I stood erect, breathing easily, staring straight ahead. I felt as if I could stand there forever. I had found the center of balance of my own body. As every dancer knows, this center is the key to everything. She must find it if she is to dance—and, incidentally, if she wants to walk on stilts.

I looked around. No one was there. They had left me to my practice while they went to their own pursuits. I took a step! Right foot forward. I knew I'd made a mistake. It wasn't like walking. Stilt-walking was walking with my hands.

The stilt dragged because I hadn't lifted it strongly enough. It slipped out of my grip. I fell again. Only this time it would be different. I would climb up again, push away from the wall, find my balance, and lift the stilt. When I set it down, I would be one step ahead.

I hung there wavering. I didn't know what to do. It felt strange. My body was adjusting to standing sideways. Most of my weight was on my back foot, my left foot. I had to shift my weight to lift it as well as the stilt and pivot forward past the right leg.

Instinctively, I knew that if I could do that, I would have taken more than a step. I would have taken a giant step! A coordination miracle. Not that I could put those thoughts into words. I was just a little girl grunting and sweating and having the time of her life. I was playing a game against myself. And I was winning.

The stilt dragged and I was already tottering. I tried to hold the left stilt rather than let it rip out of my hand. I tried to save the fall. How much I'd learned!

I climbed up again! I repeated the process. Getting upright away from the wall was nothing by that time. I didn't even notice when I did it. Taking the first step was accomplished with no effort on my part. My eyes were on the prize. Two steps. Three.

The day came when I no longer counted the steps. I was walking everywhere. I could jump. I could turn on one foot like a dancer. I was taller than my grandmother. I was taller than my mother, my aunt, even John.

And I was closer to getting my body under control. I'd learned to co-ordinate my hands and feet. I'd found my center of balance—and I'd had fun. I was incredibly happy.

$$\pi\pi\pi$$

As I have already said, my great-grandfather was a jeweler and a watch-maker as well as many other things. A hundred years ago in tiny towns all across the country, a man had to be a Jack-of-all-trades, Master-of-none because the number of people who would require one specific service was too small to make a living at any one. One result of this specific profession among his many others was that my mother and grandmother were very contemptuous of costume jewelry. They believed in the real thing or nothing.

After we came to the Valley, my mother talked frequently about how she wanted me to appreciate the finer things and to own beautiful things, real jewelry, even when I was a little girl. We were church-mouse poor out there on that farm, but Mother was determined. From Oklahoma she had brought with her an orange and white Angora tomcat named Frisky. Shortly thereafter she acquired a coal black Persian female with eyes the color of the emeralds in my grandmother's engagement ring. Mother named her Poko and started raising longhaired kittens with huge green eyes.

In those days add-a-pearl necklaces were quite the fashion for little girls. They began with one or two tiny real pearls on a fine gold chain. Any jeweler could add others to them for birthdays and Christmases. Mother was determined that I should have one. For every Persian kitten she sold, she added a pearl to my add-a-pearl necklace.

The kittens went fast because they were so lovable. From the minute their eyes opened, they'd been relentlessly played with, carried everywhere, dressed up in doll clothes, teased with pieces of string, feathers, balls, and yoyos. Every kitten that left the farm undoubtedly fell into an exhausted sleep by the time the buyer's car turned out of the lane. The little things probably didn't wake up properly for twenty-four hours.

Since Poko could only have so many litters of kittens, Mother branched out to tropical fish. She started with black mollies, red moons, and brick swordtails. Later she added guppies and moons and swordtails in gold and green. She ordered hybrid swordtail mollies, speckled mollies, and veil-tail guppies. They were all tropical livebearers. The sale of a breeding pair of black mollies equaled another pearl on my necklace.

She branched out into egg-layers and bubble-nesters—zebras, neon tetras, blue gouramis, pink kissing gouramis, and angelfish.

Believe it or not, I learned about sex from observing tropical fish. At a glance a male can be told from a female pretty much the same way a little boy can be told from a little girl. A pregnant gold moon had a dark swollen belly. The most time I ever spent in front of an aquarium was when my mother stocked Siamese fighting fish—bubble-nesters that come in rich colors of sapphire, emerald, and ruby. From them I learned all about courtship and mating.

The male danced in front of the female, his magnificent fins spread wide and waving like banners. His gills swelled and turned bright red. The female watched him as fascinated as I was. Then he darted in and wrapped himself around her.

Their bodies spasmed, galvanizing both fish like an electric shock. Even as a wide-eyed little girl, I was pretty galvanized myself. Then they slowly sank together to the bottom of the bowl. I didn't know anything about what was going on with all those fins in the way, but I knew it was something pretty important.

A pair of Siamese fighting fish bought too pearls.

It was turning out to be quite a necklace.

At the same time Mother was importing exotic fish, she was also going fishing in the canals and bar ditches.

As she told Mammaw, "There are seven kinds of tropical fish that live in the Rio Grande. If I can catch them and breed them, I'll make clear profit."

So, armed with a long pole and net and wearing sunhat, beach-shoes and old clothes including a long-sleeved shirt, my mother went fishing.

In those days people didn't throw cans and bottles into canals, lakes, and reservoirs. When people finished their soft drinks, they took the bottle back for their deposit. Beer generally was sold on tap although longneck brown bottles were appearing. However, it wasn't drunk in public and certainly not in the presence of ladies and children.

Neither were the Valley waterways polluted. Without heavy industry of any kind, it didn't have such a thing as industrial runoff. The poisonous insecticides like DDT and Chlordane hadn't been invented yet.

The worst an enterprising woman could get was a sunburn and mud between her toes. My mother did slip down in the water several times, but she always laughed and got right back up again.

Mammaw sat on an old quilt on the bank. She wore her sunbonnet, one of my grandfather's old shirts to cover her arms to her fingertips, and silk stockings with runs in them to cover her legs. All of her life she protected herself from the sun. Her skin was white as a lily.

Even though I stomped, begged, whined, and complained, I was condemned to play along the edge. I wasn't allowed to go in the water because I wasn't trustworthy. As Mammaw told me time and again, "Mona Dean, you never look before you leap."

Looming even larger in the decision to keep me on shore was the fact that none of us could swim a stroke.

We had packed a picnic lunch that included a big jar of iced tea. This was before the days of Styrofoam plastic coolers or portable ice-chests of any sort. Our tea was cool because Mammaw had filled the jar with a chunk of ice and wrapped it in a bath towel. Our sandwiches were homemade pimiento cheese because we didn't want to take the chance on meats or eggs spoiling.

Ever striving to put the best face on everything, Mammaw took this opportunity to create the appearance of a fancy picnic. On the old quilt she spread a pink luncheon cloth with white embroidered flowers appliquéd on it. I unpacked the sandwiches that had been wrapped in a clean dishtowel, and she opened a jar of homemade sweet and sour pickles. As we ate, we wiped our mouths on cloth napkins that matched the luncheon cloth. When we finished, we ate bananas for dessert.

Mother had bought special containers to carry home the fish. Car batteries were shipped in half-inch-thick blue-glass box-shaped jars. Glass was the only thing that battery acid couldn't eat through. It corroded everything else it touched. Mother had found a dozen empty ones in a junkyard for a half a dollar. She'd spent hours cleaning them of any residue and scouring their sides.

She'd driven all the way out to Red Fish Bay to spade up boxes of beach sand while I collected shells to decorate the jars so the fish would feel at home. Of course, she'd washed everything clean of salt.

Until I wrote this book, I never gave a thought to how hard she worked for those tiny pearls.

Mother actually did find some pretty fish. Big silver sail-fins with half-inch dorsals and thin orange and green stripes from their gills to their tails. They were a moderate success. Where she really made some money was breeding them to mollies to which they were distantly related. Her sail-fin molly was black with a big dorsal. She sold several pairs of them. And bought several pearls.

She used the battery jars as nurseries and took the shells I'd collected as well as most of my marbles to cover the bottoms for the little fish to hide among until they were big enough to escape being eaten. Mother's fish business grew until she had to buy a fifty-gallon aquarium and all sorts of pumps and purifiers. She bought fish food and she made her own.

Then gradually, she gave it up. Her friends had all the fish they wanted and she had less time and probably less energy. She was working nights at the telephone company, and I was too big for add-a-pearl necklaces.

One by one, the fish died until Mammaw and Mother finally emptied the aquariums and sold them.

Frisky was killed one night by a pack of coyotes, but Poko died of old age. The last cat we had before my grandmother became too ill to take care of it was a big gray tabby named Silver. He was Poko's great great great grandson. His lineage wasn't pure, having had some strays in his line after we moved into town, but his eyes were bright green, and he had the sweetest disposition.

One day, after my mother's death, when the time came for me to sell some of her things, I found those battery jars lined up in a row high between the rafters in the attic. Several of them still had beach sand in them and one had a little porcelain castle. All had marbles and shells for the baby fish to hide among to keep from being eaten.

The man who was helping me take them down, wanted to carry them straight out to the trash, but I would let him. They were dusty and laced with cobwebs, but I knew I had to say good-bye to them. In my mind's eye I could see picnics beside the canal with my grandmother's appliquéd luncheon cloth. I could see bright sapphire, emerald, and ruby Siamese fighting fish, and a delicate pearl necklace.

I could see my mother's courage, her spirit, her desire to instill in me a love and appreciation of what she called the finer things of life.

VII
TEACHERS

In the summer of 1940, I was desperately eager to start to school. Mother had told me that I would start in September when I was five going on six. I would be able to read what I were sure were real books that would be somehow different from the ones I had at home.

I'm sure I thought that I would go to school the first day and come home with my arms full of books like the ones my mother read. Since reading was the third most important thing I did after swinging through the salt cedars and walking around on stilts, I couldn't wait.

I should report that the books I had around the house were not the ones most pre-school children encounter today. They weren't even ordinary for children of my time. That is not to say that I didn't have a copy of "'Twas the Night Before Christmas," brightly illustrated. I also had "Wee Willie Winkie" by Kipling and "The Blue Bird" from the old French Fairy Tale. Winkie won my heart because he rode his pony into danger to save the Lady and then faced the Afghanis bravely. Still I had only a few books that had actually been bought for me.

Most of my pre-school learning had come from the school readers. They were part of a collection that dated back before the turn of the century. Books used to be very precious objects, purchased for a lifetime. They were bound in cloth or leather. Their folios were sewn together and then stitched and glued to the spine. The paper was of excellent quality and survives to this day yellowed but not so much that every letter and every illustration is not crystal clear.

Children in Arkansas in my grandmother's day had to buy their schoolbooks. Because they were respected, they were not discarded. Instead they were handed around. A good serviceable reader or arithmetic book could go from hand to hand through a clan. Many times my books had the name of their first owner on the flyleaf. Beneath his name would be his next brother, then his sister, then a cousin, and then a son or daughter. I was so proud when I learned to print so I could add my name. In some cases it would be the fourth or fifth name in the list.

The books my mother and grandmother read to me were, therefore, text-books with stories that increased my vocabulary and gave things to think about and talk about as Mammaw encouraged me to do. I particularly remember one poem to teach me to be gentle and respectful of my elders.

She was an old, old, old, old lady,
And the boy had a twisted knee,
And the game that they were playing
Was wonderful to see—

At first Mammaw read the stories to me. Then I read them for myself. Perhaps they didn't keep me on the "straight and narrow," but certainly I knew when I stepped off. Then my conscience would bother me.

My grandmother's gentle, "Oh, Mona Dean, aren't you sorry for what you've done?" used to make me cringe inside and out. She would remind me of the characters in the stories. My shame was total. I knew I was a bad girl. Because of the exemplum stories, I knew what was good and what was bad.

Ruth and I often discussed how we'd much rather have a switching from my own salt cedars than a talking to. Salt cedars make surprisingly effective switches considering how soft their needles are.

The night before I was to go to school, I could hardly sleep. Mother had made me a new dress for the occasion. It was blue, my favorite color, with smocking on the yoke. I had new socks and shoes. I had a lunchbox.

I was ready. I was dancing up and down I was so ready.

Mrs. Adeline Pittman, the principal of Robert E. Lee Elementary School, who'd refused to hire my mother as a teacher, stared at me as I were some particularly ugly bug and announced that she wouldn't accept a child under six. I was seven weeks short of that birthday and exceptionally tall for my age. Moreover, I could read and write.

I was refused admittance.

Mrs. Pittman was within her rights by the strict letter of Texas law that stated no child under six should go to school, but Mother knew that exceptions had been made for years for the slimmest of reasons. The general practice was, if the class wasn't crowded and the parents wanted the child in, then she could go.

Mother didn't believe for one minute that the first grade at Raymondville was too crowded. She told me to go wait in the hall. I clutched my lunchbox and clung to the wall, feeling sick at my stomach and sure that everybody was staring at me.

When Mother came out, her face was flaming. Her breath was coming short and her jaw was set. She caught me by the hand, and we practically ran down the hall. I had never been so scared.

At home she sent me out to play in the salt cedars while she told Mammaw all about what happened. I sat on the swing board and tried not to cry. I'd been counting so hard on going to school.

Then Mother brought me in. She explained that I was too young, but I was not to worry. We would go to San Perlita, a much smaller school, tomorrow and I would get to start.

I didn't find out what really happened until later. Mrs. Pittman seemed determined to keep me from starting school one day sooner than she absolutely had to let me in.

From Mrs. Pittman's point of view, my mother hadn't suffered enough. She hadn't starved and paid for her sin of divorce. She'd gone to work for the telephone company. She'd become a "Hello, Girl." My mother's job had convinced Mrs. Pittman that she'd been right all along. Mother was no good. If the truth were known, I probably wasn't even legitimate. No one had ever seen my father. I probably didn't have one. She might have to let me in next year, but if my mother wanted to do the right thing, she would take me and go back where we came from.

The next morning Mother drove out to San Perlita, rehearsing me all the way.

"How old are you, Mona Dean?"

"I'm six years old."

I slumped in the seat. Mother was asking me to tell a lie. But only for six weeks.

"When is your birthday?"

"August twenty-second."

My birthday was actually October 22. I hoped I could remember. I realized I was going to have to practice and practice in my spare time so if anybody asked me, I wouldn't blurt out the wrong date.

Mother took me into the schoolhouse. Because classes were already in session, we went straight to principal's office. I never got a chance to tell a lie. Mrs. Pittman had beaten us. She'd called the principal out there. I was not to be admitted. There was no discussion.

Mother drove home ferociously angry. That night she and Mammaw discussed the problem in front of me. Their conversation was probably the first one of an adult nature I was privy to.

"Just look at her," my mother raged. "She's tall enough to be a second or a third grader. She can read anything we put in front of her. She can print. She writes page-long letters to her Granddad Tom."

I nodded enthusiastically. I really could do all those things and I really wanted to learn to do more.

"They can't deny her," Mother went on. "This child has to start to school."

"You can't drive her to Harlingen and work too," Mammaw said. "It would be too far." Harlingen was in Cameron County where even the redoubtable Mrs. Pittman would have no power. The trip would be more than fifty miles twice a day.

"But she has to start school," Mother nearly wailed. "If we wait till next year, she'll be so tall, she'll be a freak. And she'll be bored to tears. She can't start in the first grade when she's six going on seven."

I nodded again. Ruth was already in the second grade. Being almost a year and a half older than I, she was year ahead of me in school. I was so ready and I had been promised I could go this year. I would have friends to play with, and many new books to read.

So Mother looked at a map of Willacy County and took me still farther afield. For some reason Mrs. Pittman had not remembered Willamar, a four-room schoolhouse for farmers' children on the easternmost farm-to-market road in Willacy County. Between Willamar and the Gulf of Mexico lay nothing more than a few miles of cotton fields and salt marshes.

Mother drove me there rehearsing me again to say that I was six and my birthday was August 22. As it happened I didn't even have to tell my little lie. I didn't even stay the day in the first grade. Since I'd come in late, the teacher gave me an oral test as I stood beside her desk.

First she asked me to name the colors.

I started to name as many as I could remember. "Red, blue, blue-green, yellow-green, aquamarine, tan, pink, rose, black, brown, sienna, gold, orange . . ."

The teacher stopped me.

I was glad. I didn't think I could remember all thirty-two of them from the giant Crayola box.

She asked me if I knew the alphabet.

I tipped back my head and sang it like a bird. I thought it was supposed to be sung. She opened the reader to the back. I read the last story aloud. I printed my name for her. She took a good look at me. I fidgeted waiting for the next question, but she didn't even ask my age.

I was placed in the second grade.

Those old readers had taught me. Those old books and my grandmother who read to me for countless hours and then listened for countless hours as I read the books back to her. We discussed each story, even if for only a few sentences. I often wonder what would have happened had I stayed home for Mammaw to educate.

πππ

I would like to tell you that I had an idyllic time in the second grade at Willamar, but I didn't. Instead, I found myself in a school of hard knocks where I was pummeled and prodded into becoming a social human being.

The first grade contained only first graders who had to be taught how to read and cooperate with each other. I didn't even have Ruth to support me at Willamar. When I was put into the second grade, I was one of a dozen who were expected to do work on their own. The teacher expected that we also would know how to cooperate with each other.

To make matters worse or better, Miss Ferguson's room also contained eight third graders, and six fourth graders, and six fifth graders. All of us second graders were regarded as babies who made all sorts of dumb mistakes all the time.

I was in a hard spot. I had never been around so many children, especially older children. I had been the cherished one, the praised one, the *only* one. I didn't know how to cooperate. I didn't know how to behave when I wasn't the center of attention.

Moreover, even though I was now the total care of Vora Bevens and Hona Young, I was also Fred Young's daughter. The bad temper that characterized my father at his worst was also my temper. The inevitable result of being an only child was an impossibly spoiled little girl who thought she was smarter than anyone else. I was headed for trouble.

I was only five. All of my classmates were from seven to ten and even eleven. I was very much younger and very immature. I couldn't even blow my own nose. I didn't always understand what the teacher was asking of me. I had a choice as to how I would conduct myself. I could be a baby and cry all the time. Or I could erect a façade and hide behind it. I chose to wrap myself in pride.

For instance, when Miss Ferguson called the roll, I answered "President" because I thought the others weren't pronouncing the word correctly. All the students laughed, but I thought they were wrong and I was right.

Oh, I was arrogant as only a spoiled and treasured only child can be!

Then a fifth grader at recess told me very rudely to say, "Present, Dummy. It means 'here.'"

I was flabbergasted, then embarrassed. I could feel hot blood run into my cheeks. Even my ears turned hot. I wanted to fly at that girl and hit her and kick her and knock her down. I clenched my fingers to keep from grabbing her hair. My teeth champed like a cat's. I wanted her neck.

Instead, I made myself walk stiffly into the restroom. I sat on the toilet for the rest of recess. I was shaking and angry and then embarrassed all over again. I wanted to cry, but I wouldn't let myself. I somehow knew that would be the worst thing I could do.

At home that afternoon I perched in the salt cedars and pouted. I didn't tell Mammaw my mistake. She would be disappointed in me. I brooded. I tried without success to get sick. I failed. How I hated my blooming good health!

None of my ploys made any difference. In the morning I had to go back to school. I didn't speak to anyone on the playground because I knew they wouldn't want to speak to me. I had made a mistake. I hated myself. I didn't want to admit that I was wrong, but everyone knew. I was the object of scorn with my very public mistake.

When the teacher called the roll, I almost didn't answer. My face turned red all over again. I wanted to cry. I wanted to hide. I clutched the sides of the desk. "Here," I whispered.

The fifth grader laughed. Her friends laughed. I was thoroughly humiliated and furiously angry. I hated to be wrong. I was certain no one would ever like me again.

I had come to believe that being right was the only way to be a success. It was the only way people in this terrible school would respect me. I had to be respected. I had to be right.

Otherwise, I would starve. I would be poor. I would be condemned forever to the lowest level of human existence. Moreover, people wouldn't like me if I were poor and always making mistakes. Only if I were perfect would people like me. Only by deserving people's respect and friendship could I win it.

Where did I come by this conviction?

Despite everything Mammaw could do to put a good face on our life on the farm, I was aware that times were very bad. Every garment that I wore was homemade except my shoes and underpants. I had only three pairs of socks that I wore only on cold days.

We canned food all through the sweltering summers. Corn, tomatoes, green beans, carrots, black-eyed peas. We made and canned vegetable soup with chicken. When our situation grew desperate, Mammaw arranged to trade water from our well for a locker at Brenner's grocery.

We butchered a calf and paid Mr. Brenner to cut it, wrap it, and freeze it. Then when Mother and Mammaw would go into town on Saturday, they'd go by the grocery store and bring home the packages wrapped in white paper, tied with string and labeled with a wax crayon.

I knew all about this. From it I drew a dim, largely unfocused conclusion. Somehow things had gone wrong in the lives of my mother and grandmother. They couldn't earn a good living. They expected better things of me. I had to learn. I had to get an education. I couldn't make mistakes because then people wouldn't like me.

Moreover, I knew that my mother had made a mistake by divorcing my father. People like Mrs. Pittman didn't like her. If they didn't like me, they would take what I had away from me because I didn't deserve it.

Such was my convoluted thinking.

Of course, I went on to make mistakes, and people liked me well enough I suppose. I had a few friends. Some like Ruth have stayed with me all my life. But the underlying fear kept me from getting too close. I wasn't worthy of friendship because I would always make mistakes no matter how hard I tried not to.

Even today the old responses govern my life. I'll go to Herculean lengths to keep from exposing any weakness. It's made me wary—an over-achiever at anything requiring competent execution.

I'm frequently surprised to find people think I'm stuck up. They'd be amazed to learn that my greatest fear is that they'll somehow discover and think less of me because I couldn't tell the difference between "president" and "present" when I was five years old.

$$\pi\pi\pi$$

Mother arranged for me to have a ride home from Willamar School with Thalia Gayle Smith. My mother would take the two of us girls to school. Every morning she drove seven miles east toward the Gulf of Mexico, then fourteen miles back west to Raymondville before she went to work at the telephone office. People today think little of such a drive, but then it was a great sacrifice of time and strength with cars that had stiff standard transmissions and neither power brakes nor steering.

Thalia Gayle's mother would pick us up in the afternoon as soon as school was out.

This arrangement worked well for both women because driving made Helen nervous, and she didn't like to be rushed. Also she wore glasses and didn't like to drive east into the morning sun or into the dimness of early morning in November.

Everything went according to plan until one afternoon a hurricane blew in.

In 1940 no television broadcasts with information from satellites tracked hurricanes for days before they actually made landfall. The weathermen would try to predict the weather over the radio, but mostly they were wrong. Hurricanes didn't even have names and no one really bothered to keep track of them. When the wind was high, the Coast Guard posted small craft warnings on the bays and marinas. Nothing more. People on land were pretty much on their own.

So Mother drove us to school that morning and left, aware only that the day was very still and very hot even for the sub-tropical Valley.

Soon after she left, the wind began to blow and the rain began to slant in from the east. The sky turned bruise purple with yellow streaks. Rain gusted across the schoolyard and hit the windows in sheets. We didn't go out for recess and we ate our lunches at our desks. The lights went out. Miss Ferguson read to all of us second, third, fourth, and fifth graders from a chair by the window.

The rain kept pouring down. The swings blew up and over the A-frames. The school-ground flooded. Water washed over the lowest of the front steps. Mrs. Brandt, the teacher-principal, sent the few children who lived close enough to the school to wade home.

In the classroom we got wilder and wilder. Every time a gust would hit, the girls would shudder, and the boys would hiss and punch each other. The time drew near for school to be out. A few fathers who lived along the paved road came in pickups to take their children home. We all began to worry when only one of our two buses showed up.

The driver who came wasn't sure he could make it, but he was willing to try. Of course, all of his load were anxious to get home. Mrs. Brandt sent them dashing across the school-ground in groups of four under the only two umbrellas in the school. She was loading only three children at a time because otherwise they'd be soaked.

We all watched from the window of Miss Ferguson's room as the driver and our lucky classmates pulled out in his big yellow bus. Behind him, he left a white wake that came rolling toward us like water up a beach.

The rest of us were marched into the common room that served as an assembly and recreation area since we had no gymnasium.

I watched the hands crawl around the face of the schoolhouse clock. Even though I wasn't too certain about how to tell time, when five o'clock came and went, my stomach told me loud and clear.

At that time we learned the school had absolutely nothing to feed us. I had devoured everything Mammaw had packed for me at lunch. The sandwich, the apple, and the chocolate cookie were merely fond memories. My thermos of Kool-Aid was empty too.

Thalia Gayle had four small tangerines left over from lunch. She'd picked them herself from her tree in her front yard. She shared them with me and two of her other friends. They didn't help at all. My stomach didn't like being empty.

The room was bare and dim except for chairs to sit in and a piano. We were too upset and excited to stay seated for very long. Mostly, we milled around, some of the girls crying, most of the boys roughhousing. I can only imagine what the three teachers were going through.

And I have to remember them with gratitude at this time. They stayed with us at their posts when they could have gotten in their cars and driven home. I doubt very seriously if any among them had a thought about leaving us.

The rain kept sheeting against the windows. The thunder had rolled on through, but the wind howled constantly. The teachers lighted kerosene lamps and a few candles, but generally we were in the dark, hungry, scared and miserable.

Mrs. Brandt proposed a talent show. Miss Ferguson played the piano and everyone sang everything he knew. I remember I did the tap dance from my last recital. Hop-shuffle-step, shuffle-ball-change. Hop-shuffle-step, shuffle-ball-change. But my heart wasn't in it.

I wanted to go home.

It was totally dark. We were going to have to sleep on the floor, boys on one side, girls on the other. I didn't want to cry, but Thalia Gayle had been weeping for several minutes.

Then the door opened.

My mother stood there—wet to the skin, hair streaming, her feet bare and muddy. Behind her was John, our hired man. I ran to her and hugged her hard. She lifted me in her arms and looked me straight in the eye. Her face was white and very wet. Her naturally curly hair was plastered to her forehead and cheeks in fishhooks. I swallowed and hugged her again.

Mrs. Brandt came hurrying to us. "Mrs. Young, how did you get here?"

"Over the railroad track," Mother said. Then she put me down. "Get your book satchel."

When I brought it, she took off my shoes and socks and put them in it. She took off Thalia Gayle's shoes and socks and put them in hers. Mrs. Brandt hovered above us.

"What are the roads beyond the tracks like?"

"I couldn't see a thing," Mother said. "Not the shoulder, not the white line. The water's over the road."

Mrs. Brandt's mouth dropped open. She shook her head. She must have known that probably no other parents would be there that night.

Even as she turned away, my mother picked me up. John picked up Thalia Gayle, and we went out into the night. I put my arms around Mother's neck and clapped my cheek tight against hers as the wind and rain hit us in the face. We slitted our eyes, so we could see.

She slogged through water to her knees all the way across the playground and through a narrow field of new-planted winter onions, under water, undoubtedly a total loss to the farmer. Down into the railroad ditch, she waded through water so deep my feet trailed in it. Here my mother staggered. She bent her body into the wind and then trudged up onto the tracks.

For a few seconds she stood there, breathing hard. Cold rain pelted us. Then she put me down. John still carried Thalia Gayle, but I took my Mother's hand and we walked together carefully over the slippery crossties. Water sluiced over the gravel between them and ran into the ditches on either side.

I could see the headlights of the car on the turnoff up ahead. Mother had parked it across the road, so the lights would guide us back.

I was almost too numb to care when Mother and John put us girls in the front seat. Then she climbed in and started the car. John waded to the side of the road, to show her where it was until she could get turned around. Then we started home.

John held Thalia Gayle and I sat pressed against my mother's hip, one leg on each side of the gearshift. As we started, I looked back toward the school. It was lost in the pelting rain. All I could see was water. It flowed out behind us like the white wake of a boat.

How Mother got us home, I didn't stay awake to see. I settled down with my head in her lap. The car heater was blowing full blast. I was warm and safe.

At long last we drove up to the back door of our house. When Mother turned the motor off, both of us girls woke up. Mother was leaning on the steering wheel, still clutching it with both hands, still staring straight ahead. She didn't even offer to take Thalia Gayle home. She would spend the night with me.

Mammaw had a hot supper ready, but her eyes were red and wet. I wondered if she had a cold. I never considered that she'd been weeping in fear for her daughter and granddaughter. "How did you do it?" she asked.

Mother shook her head as if she didn't know herself. "By the palms," she said. "By the palm trees. They're about twenty feet off the road."

The next morning Thalia Gayle's father came by on his tractor to tell Mammaw and Mother he was going to get us. When his own daughter ran out to meet him, his mouth dropped open. He couldn't believe that Mother had brought us home in the storm in a Chevrolet. He hadn't even tried to go out the evening before.

"Why that was dangerous," he said.

If it had been left to him, his five-year-old daughter would have spent the night with the rest of Willamar's children in the dark schoolhouse without food or blankets. Or in the school bus stuck and stranded on a back road.

My mother's courage and determination brought us home, dried us off, fed us, and put us to bed. Rain, flood, thunder, and lightning never stopped Hona Bevens Young. Not where I was concerned. She was an absolute certainty in my life.

From that moment on, I never could bring myself to disappoint her. I knew how much she loved me.

ππ π

Bleached domestic cost nineteen cents a yard. Good cotton broadcloth, thirty-six inches wide in solid colors, generally cost ten cents more. If the material was printed with little flowers or woven in plaids or checks, it cost another five cents. Most of my dresses cost forty-five cents apiece. Everything would have been all right if Mammar had only stopped there.

Her father-in-law, old W. R. Bevens, had owned a general store as well as a bank that failed and sections of land from land grants issued and signed by Presidents James Buchanan, Abraham Lincoln, and Andrew Johnson. Every so often she would show me the grants, so I would know about them and know that we had always been landed gentry.

When W. R. died and the general store closed, Mammaw inherited all the rickrack braid, bias tape, laces, ribbons, buttons, and silk and cotton threads that were left unsold.

I hadn't been in the classroom more than a few days before I noticed that none of the other girls' hair was tied back with a big moiré taffeta bow. Neither was their hair elaborately curled. None of their dresses looked like they were made from Butterick patterns.

No. I was the *only* child in Willamar with dresses that could be called pretty. I wish I could say I was proud or even appreciative, but I hated those dresses.

Why? Because they made me different from the first day. My clothes also fit me perfectly because Mammaw was an excellent seamstress. Moreover, because I was an only child, I wore no faded, worn garments passed down from the oldest until they finally ended up on the baby sister.

My dresses were trimmed with all manner of cunning notions. Their hems were hemstitched on a professional double-needle machine. My grandmother owned the only one in the Rio Grande Valley, a relic of bygone prosperity. The ruffled edges of my collars and sleeves were picoted, and my seams were piped or faggoted. My yokes were smocked and embroidered and appliquéd. On patchwork pockets bloomed rickrack flowers with button centers.

When I stormed and whined and complained bitterly, Mammaw looked hurt or perhaps exasperated. But not deterred. With quiet purpose she tied my sashes in the back. She continued to curl my hair and comb it back. Though I "lost" several ribbons in the brush at the edge of the schoolyard, she seemed to have an inexhaustible supply of moiré taffeta.

I might be poor now, she seemed to say, but I was special. I would look my *specialness*.

It was the stuff of tragedy.

Five years old in the second grade was bad enough. Thalia Gayle had been put in the first grade, but I had been "placed" in the second grade. I could already read well above grade level and when called upon to read, I read "with expression" instead of in a stumbling monotone. I was a stranger in a four-room schoolhouse where no one dressed anywhere near as well as I did. As a consequence they all looked at me as if they hated me.

At least some of them probably did. I didn't know they were sharecropper's children, most of them from big families. In two cases brothers and sisters sat side by side in different grades. The boys uniformly wore overalls or khaki work pants. Some of the girls wore dresses made of flour-sacks. Almost everyone wore hand-me-downs, faded and frayed. Some clothes looked as if they hadn't been ironed.

Even worse problems arose with my lunches.

Since Willamar had no cafeteria to serve a hot meal even if anyone could have afforded one, we all carried sack lunches. Except me. Mammaw seemed to think I was having a picnic every day. She had bought me a tin lunch pail with a puppy and a kitten on it. It had a thermos bottle filled with Kool-Aid or hot chocolate depending on the season.

She trimmed the crusts off my bread and cut my sandwiches diagonally. She sliced a fresh tomato and folded salt into a two-inch square of wax paper. She included special store-bought devil's food cookies dipped in chocolate. She scored the orange peel down the sides and lifted the corners, so I could peel it easily. She packed a paper napkin.

My sufferings were unimaginable.

Everyone looked at those devil's food cookies as if they were gold. Only when we would have picnics and everyone would share their lunches did the other girls seem to like me.

I didn't think things could possibly get any worse, but the final stroke was yet to come.

At the end of the year, the entire school—probably sixty people and three teachers—had a special night. All the eighth graders—only nine students—were leaving Willamar forever. Four would go to high school in Raymondville, but for five this would be their last year of formal schooling. They would go to work beside their fathers or stay home and help their mothers until they got married and had families of their own.

This was their last night to shine, to show off what they had learned. Without exception they spoke their pieces. The girl who had made best grades was named. One girl sang a duet with her sister, a seventh grader.

Then came the rest of the students. Some recited. The fourth and fifth grade sang two songs Miss Ferguson had taught them. The first graders also sang—very badly.

I looked down the purple hectographed program. Gradually, horror began to dawn on me. Again, I was the only one. *The only one.* I was to play my recital piece "Little Dutch Dance" on the piano. I was the only one in the whole school taking private lessons.

On leaden feet I trudged over to the scarred upright. I sat down. The full skirt of my pussy-willow silk dress flared out about me. Mammaw had made it from the skirt of one of Mother's Chicago dresses, a touch of vanished opulence. I looked at my mother and Mammaw sitting there. They were smiling. I could see such pride in my grandmother's face.

I couldn't disappoint them. No matter how unhappy I was, I couldn't let them know it.

I lifted my hands to the keyboard. The little waltz rippled out without a single mistake. When I was finished, I rose and dropped a curtsey just as my piano teacher had told me to do. Then while everyone applauded, I came back and sat down. Mother scooted over so I could sit between them. She patted my leg. I felt Mammaw's hand adjust a curl in my hair.

To this day, I'm so glad I didn't disappoint them.

πππ

Even though I loved Miss Ferguson at Willamar, I had now passed my sixth birthday, so that I could legally go to school in Texas. I no longer had to tell everybody that my birthday was August twenty-second. I could ride the bus to school and save Mother a long drive in the mornings.

To start my second year in school, Mother brought me back to try to enroll me in the third grade at Robert E. Lee Elementary School in Raymondville.

Unfortunately, the person she had to face was Mrs. Pittman, all the more ferocious and resentful because Mother had managed to win a round in their battle.

I will never forget that woman so long as I live. She had wavy iron gray hair combed back from a gaunt angular face. Her hair was cut short and covered by a very fine gray hairnet. Not one hair could stray no matter how high the wind. Her forehead was high, her eyebrows gray and drawn together in a perpetual frown. Her nose was a long hatchet thrusting imperiously ahead of her like the prow of a battleship. Her chin was pointed and her mouth tightly pursed.

She fixed me with a beady eye and said not a word.

I held tight to Mother's skirt while she handed over my report card and book card from Willamar. Mrs. Pittman scarcely glanced at them.

I'd made all *A*'s except in arithmetic, the mysteries of which still escape me. Mother filled out the necessary card to enroll me and left.

Clutching my book satchel and lunchbox, I was marched into a classroom with a 2B card taped beside the door. The teacher issued my books. I recognized every one of them. They were books I'd read at Willamar. They were the books that saved me. Although I was terribly afraid, I found my voice.

"I've read these," I said.

The look Mrs. Pittman shot me almost paralyzed me.

I said no more, but I was shaking.

Only one other person looked as uncomfortable as I did. Byrne James was new to Raymondville, and he was a few weeks older than I was. Mrs. Pittman had stowed him in the second grade too although he'd gone to the second grade elsewhere.

I went home that night and showed all my books to Mammaw and Mother. This time they didn't say anything where I could hear them, but the next day Mother went back with me.

She sent me back to the second grade, and she went into Mrs. Pittman's office. Mrs. Pittman adamantly refused to move me. I was only six years old. The second grade was divided into high and low for the older and younger students. I belonged in the low second grade with the younger children.

Mother walked out and marched straight to the Willacy County Superintendent of Schools, Mr. Brandt, whose wife was the sixth, seventh, and eighth grade teacher at Willamar. Mother asked for a placement test. She agreed to abide by whatever score I made.

I think that if Mother's had been the only protest, she would probably have failed, but the Jameses had come to see the superintendent too. Faced with two complaints among maybe fifty students, he threw up his hands. He said he would overrule his principal only on condition that our scores showed proficiency of second grade material.

Byrne and I took a special test together.

After we'd finished, we all sat waiting in the outer office while Mr. Brandt graded the tests himself. Then he called in the Jameses. They came out all smiles. Mrs. James hugged Byrne, Mr. James smiled at Mother and me, and they went away.

Then Mr. Brandt signaled to Mother. He took her into the office while I had to wait nervously outside. She told me later what he said. I had tested as proficient through the fifth grade, fourth month. He said that he didn't think Mother would want me in the fifth grade at six years of age.

Would the high third do?

Smiling like the Cheshire cat, Mother agreed. She hugged me hard and took me out for a nickel ice cream cone. All the way home, she kept patting me.

I was not really surprised at the news. I didn't think I'd done such a great thing. I didn't think the test was hard—just long. I wish I could remember how long I worked. Probably no more than an hour, certainly not two, but I was exhausted. At six I'd never taken a test so long. In fact, to tell the truth, I got too tired to answer some of the questions at the very end.

But it was everything I had learned at Willamar in the classroom with second, third, fourth, and fifth grade all together—in reading, spelling, arithmetic and geography.

I had made an excellent score on the standard achievement test for elementary school—the test students were supposed to take before they moved on to junior high. In fact, if I had been in the fifth grade, I would have been passed on to the sixth.

The next day Mrs. Pittman came for us. Byrne and I were moved into Mrs. Davis's room. Mrs. Pittman told Mrs. Davis in an icy voice, "This is Hona Young's daughter."

Mrs. Davis looked at me from under a head of bright red hair, the color of a brush fire. I'd never seen hair that color before nor skin that white. Her mouth tightened. I was scared to death. I knew she didn't like me. I never thought of her as anyone other than Mrs. "Red-Haired" Davis.

When I brought my report card home after the first six weeks, my grades were absolutely average. I had made nothing but C's. C's in reading although I could read every word in the texts and answer all the questions. My hand was always up first. I loved to answer first and show off. I was still wrapped in my fierce, protective pride.

I made C's in geography studies although I loved to read about children in faraway lands and I could color maps and stay inside the lines. C's in spelling although I also made one hundred every week, and Mammaw saw that I memorized all the rules and could apply them. *C*'s in arithmetic. Those I probably deserved. That was the one thing Mammaw hadn't taught me.

At one Parent-Teacher Association meeting, my mother asked Mrs. Davis why I had a *C* in spelling. We had long slim spelling tablets with enough pages for the entire year, so my mother could look back and see the one hundred every week.

Mrs. Davis looked down at me and then she looked up at Mother. Her mouth tightened and she looked away. In a low voice, as if she were telling a secret, she said, "Nobody can take what she knows away from her, can they?"

Then she closed her mouth and turned away. I looked up at Mother. She looked down at me. I nodded solemnly. I knew what Mrs. Davis was saying. I could understand it too. It was what Mammaw always said about education being the one thing nobody could take away from me. What I didn't understand was why Mrs. Davis said it to me, and why my mother looked as if she were about to cry.

I was really sad. I saw how disappointed my mother was. Of course, in my naiveté I didn't understand what Mrs. Davis was really saying.

After that night, my mother didn't go to another PTA meeting. In fact she stayed strictly away from the school. She told me she really didn't have time with her work schedule, but she always looked at my report cards though the grades stayed the same for the rest of year, she always kissed me and told me how smart I was.

Not until years later was I able to put two and two together and figure out that Mrs. Pittman might have had a hand in determining my grades. Even then I was an adult before I fully understood about the clash of wills that caught Mrs. Davis in the middle, about one minister's daughter's extreme moral prejudice, and about how wretched my mother felt about the injustice that tormented her innocent daughter.

ππ π

Before I actually went to school, I had taught myself to read. Mammaw started out pointing to each word and turning the pages. So I too pointed and turned the pages at the proper time. I can't remember when I took the great leap—probably akin to a beginning pilot taking his first solo flight. But quite suddenly, seemingly over night, I could read.

By the time I was seven, I had memorized every book on the farm that was suitable for me to read. It was absolutely painless and such a joy. Soon

Mammaw was taking the books out of my hand and sending me out to play for fear that I wouldn't get enough exercise.

Our small home library was soon exhausted.

Mother had expected that I would have books when I went to Willamar, but, alas, the small school had no library. Even Robert E. Lee Elementary in Raymondville had only one small room with books on low shelves.

The first time I checked out a book there, I took it back to the classroom, read it all sitting at my desk, and asked to go back to return it and borrow another. Mrs. "Red-Haired" Davis refused to let me go, so I had to wait a week for another book. I didn't really blame her. I thought I should have picked a harder book that would have taken me longer to read.

When I came home and told Mother and Mammaw, they looked at each other with that look that told me they weren't telling me something, but they were telling each other volumes. What they were saying was that we had to find another book source. Otherwise, my thirst for knowledge wouldn't be satisfied. Neither the town of Raymondville nor the county of Willacy had a library.

Mother came home and told Mammaw that the nearest library was in Harlingen in the next county twenty-seven miles away. She was told that we could check out as many as ten books at a time. I could have five and Allen could have five. Ten books every two weeks. I was so excited I jumped up and down and begged to go right then.

The only problem was that Mother couldn't take us. By that time she was working Saturdays and Sundays at the telephone company because those hours paid better.

Mammaw would have to take us. No other choice was possible as she saw it. By that time I was reading aloud to Allen, who was three. Both of her grandchildren must have their education. Education was, after all, the one thing that no one could take away from them.

Mammaw hadn't driven in years. She'd been afraid that her arm, damaged by the radical mastectomy, was too weak to steer the car while she shifted the gears. But we had to have books. For us, she would force herself.

So we set out in the old Chevrolet—two children and one very nervous, but very determined lady.

We found the Harlingen Public Library in a small building on a residential street. Actually it was only a long L-shaped room to one side of the main door. The other side of the building was rented out to offices, as I remember.

When we entered, the librarian was very kind. She pointed me to the children's section. I had never seen so many books, but I knew I was equal to the challenge. I was very methodical. I started with the A's—Andy Adams's *Log of a Cowboy* and Bess Streeter Aldrich's *A Lantern in her Hand*.

I read and read and read. Allen couldn't read yet, so when I wasn't reading silently, I was reading aloud to him. As I've said before, Mother, who had an Associate of Arts degree in music and speech, encouraged me to "read with expression." I read for hours and hours. A hundred, hundred, hundred words about children and and their adventures in the adult world far removed from the farm and Raymondville.

Mother watched with pleasure. She too read constantly in her spare time. And she loved to own books. Not content with letting me simply borrow books, Mother wanted me to have the joy of owning them as well. To that end she bought *The Bobbsey Twins* and *Nancy Drew*. Several dozen each.

They were full-sized books but with pasteboard covers rather than cloth-bindings. I read them over and over, getting dirty finger-marks on the card-board backs and sometimes spattering food on the pages when I carried them away to read in the salt cedars with a piece of fruit or an Oreo for suste-nance.

Because the Bobbseys and Nancy were series books and not "good litera-ture," Mother subscribed to the Junior Literary Guild for me. Once a month I'd receive in the post office box a selection from the very best literature being written for children.

In a time when my mother's salary was less than twenty-five dollars a week, she was spending two or three dollars a month on books for me, eight dollars a month for my private piano lessons, and five dollars a month for my dance lessons. We were too poor for anything but the barest necessities, but so far as she was concerned, education was not a luxury.

I was being intensively and extensively educated. My mind and body never rebelled. Acquisitive child that I was, I truly believed that education was the one thing that nobody could take away from me, and I have never had cause to doubt it.

πππ

I have other dreary memories of my year in the third grade under the icy eye of Mrs. Davis. I felt very uncomfortable from the very first because, in effect, I had to start school over again. Instead of getting to move across the aisle into the third grade as I would have if I'd stayed in Miss Ferguson's class at Willamar, I had to make new friends. With the exception of Ruth Warren and a brief time spent in the second grade with Byrne James, I didn't know anybody.

Moreover, I knew I wasn't wanted in Mrs. Davis's class. Even though I'd taken a test that proved I was smart enough to be there, I couldn't forget that no one wanted me. I was miserable. I wanted so much to be liked.

Mrs. Davis was scary. Her hair was so red that the skin beneath it was sometimes red. I observed this phenomenon without realizing that she used a powerful henna rinse on it. Incidentally, I also observed that Mrs. Pittman's iron gray hair had a definite blue cast to it on occasion. I didn't remember Mrs. Ferguson or Mrs. Brandt at Willamar having such strange colors in their hair. I began to be afraid that the two women I had to see almost everyday were not human somehow. Certainly they weren't like anyone else I knew.

I dreaded walking to and from recess because I was afraid of seeing Mrs. Pittman patrolling the hallway. Because I was so much taller than all the other children, my head always stuck up over the others in the line. At the very sight of me, her mouth would purse as if she'd eaten a very sour pickle.

Instead of getting in my mother's car and being driven to school, I now had to ride the bus, but for some reason the bus no longer came by in front of the salt cedars as it had done since we'd lived there. It took another route that meant that I had to walk more than a quarter of a mile down a dirt road to my bus stop.

On days when rain muddied the road, Mammaw would walk with me, carrying my shoes and socks, a towel, and a pail of water. At the highway, she'd wash my feet, dry them off, and get me dressed to catch the bus.

I truly don't remember much about Mrs. Davis's class except how frustrated I was and how frightened. After a day of trying to understand what she was saying, I'd ride the bus to our farm road and trudge home. It really wasn't a long walk, but I was a little kid.

The walk gave me time to dwell on my mistakes and try to figure out what I didn't know. I was so intimidated by Mrs. Davis's red hair that I wouldn't ask for help.

Fortunately, I brought my books home every single night and Mammaw explained everything to me. We practiced my handwriting that looked terrible in comparison to my classmates'. Looking back, I think my handwriting to this day looks very much like my grandmother's, very spiky and staccato rather than looping and graceful.

Mammaw called out my spelling words until I knew every one and could rattle them off pronouncing each syllable as I spoke.

"Together. T-o-to g-e-ge t-h-e-r-ther. Together." I won every spelling bee until Mrs. Davis stopped having them. I hated that she did. It was the only thing I thought I was really good at.

Mammaw taught me not to like arithmetic, just the way she'd been taught. Still, I recited the multiplication tables as fast as my tongue could twist around them. My favorites were ones, fives, and tens. Those I understood. But sevens were a disaster. Why was seven times seven forty-nine? Fifty would have been so much easier to remember. Why was nine times three twenty-seven while seven times four was twenty-eight? I didn't understand arithmetic. I just memorized it.

Mammaw taught me to love history and to read it with real joy. She drilled me on my dates and definitions. She sat with me while I colored my maps and learned to spell the oceans and the continents.

"Australia. A-u-s-aus t-r-a-tra l-i-a-ya. Australia."

I went back to school every day armed to the teeth, but I never earned a smile. Fortunately, thanks in part to Ruth, who was always kind to me, I was also making friends and learning to be comfortable with other children who were two years older than I was.

Then came the most embarrassing moment of my entire life.

I forgot to go to the bathroom during recess. Less than an hour into the afternoon's lessons, I was in pain. I didn't dare go up to Mrs. Davis. She would look at me with that terrible stare. I was sure she wouldn't let me go anyway.

I tried to think about other things. I crossed my legs. I sat up straighter. I twisted and turned. The longer I sat, the more urgent my need became. I had to go up to her desk. But I was afraid to walk up. She'd see me coming. She'd look at me as if she wanted me to go away.

I had no idea how long before the bell. I knew I couldn't wait any longer. I was in pain. Then my pain turned to sheer terror. I realized I couldn't go up to her desk. I'd waited too long. I couldn't move.

Just before the bell rang, I lost control. So long as I live, I'll never forget the hot puddle that spread under my seat. I squeezed my legs tight, but it was no use. My little cotton panties were instantly soaked through. The back of my skirt couldn't stop it.

The urine dripped on the floor. Several people around me looked. Their noses wrinkled. They giggled. I like to think most of the class didn't know about it.

The bell rang at last. I sat like a statue. Everyone filed out. Quite a few giggled. From behind her desk at the front of the room, Mrs. Davis looked at me. Her red eyebrows rose.

"Mona Dean?" she asked.

I didn't answer. I grabbed my books and ran out, my wet dress-tail flapping against the back of my thighs.

I hid in the bathroom until the buses came. My shame was devastating. I couldn't even cry because I was so embarrassed. I sat by myself at the back of the bus. But when the bus let me out, I started crying. I cried all the way home.

From the kitchen window Mammaw saw me coming. She came out and brought me in. I was too embarrassed to tell her what was wrong, even though she knew immediately because my dress was still damp. I tried to lie and tell her that someone had thrown water on me. I didn't want my grandmother to know. She would be so disappointed in me.

Then I broke down and told the truth. Mammaw didn't scold me. She gave me a bath and told me not to worry. "It's just a little mistake," she said. "Just always remember to go to the bathroom at recess."

For the second time in my life, I didn't want to go back to school the next day. But of course, I had to. One girl asked me about it, but I just shook my head. I didn't actually tell a lie. I just didn't answer her.

I remembered after that. And the next year I had a different teacher, Miss Juanita Pollard, who had black hair like Miss Ferguson's. When she smiled at me, I knew this year was going to be different.

As a footnote to the whole wretched story, Mrs. Pittman was my teacher in the fifth grade. I didn't cower. I'd made all *A's* and *B's* in the fourth.

The first six weeks, I made all *Bs* except for one *C* in arithmetic. The second six weeks, I made *A's* in spelling and in reading. From then on I steadily improved until I was again making the Honor Roll every time. We were supposed to read a book every two weeks and report on it. Since I read many, many more than that, Mammaw encouraged me to report on everyone I read.

At the end of the last six weeks Mrs. Pittman returned all our book reports. Thick-heeled black nurses' Oxfords clacking, she stalked up and down the aisles handing the book reports out in alphabetical order. She did everything in alphabetical order, so she could record grades and pass papers out efficiently I suppose.

When she came to last two students in the room—Ginger Woods and Mona Dean Young—she held up my sheaf in one hand and three sheets of paper in the other. "This is the difference in what one student can do and what another can do," she announced in an angry voice.

With that she slapped my thirty-seven book reports down on my desk. At the same time, Mrs. Pittman dropped the three little sheets on Ginger's desktop. Ginger, who had to wear thick glasses and frequently got headaches, was so embarrassed that she hid her face. I was embarrassed too. I had been hurt so many times that I didn't want any attention called to myself, but I felt such sympathy for Ginger. I'd been in her place too. I reached across my desk and patted her shoulder.

As Mrs. Pittman stalked back down the aisle to her desk, I stuck my tongue out at her. I'd never done such a thing before. The act made me feel a little better. Such a tiny revenge.

Mrs. Pittman never really changed. She retired soon after that and died before we graduated. The school district thought so much of her that they named an elementary school after her. I thought that was the worst thing I'd ever heard of—and still do.

After I'd become a straight *A* student in high school and my name and picture appeared in the *Raymondville Chronicle, the Willacy County News,* and the *Valley Morning Star* for winning both the district-wide American Legion Oratorical Contest and the district Inter-Scholastic League Debate, Mrs. "Red-Haired" Davis saw my mother on the street one day. My former third grade teacher told Mother how proud she was of me for my accomplishments. She said she'd always known how smart I was.

Ha!

VIII
THE WAR

World War II started for me at Thalia Gayle's seventh birthday party Sunday afternoon, December 7, 1941.

Helen Smith had invited me along with a number of other girls and boys to help celebrate. Of course, no one could know how the afternoon would turn out. Not a single person there could imagine that even as we played pin-the-tail-on-the-donkey, squadrons of Japanese warplanes were attacking for the second time, strafing American warships and bases.

The official information was announced over the radio the next day when President Franklin Delano Roosevelt asked Congress to declare war. Who actually delivered the news to Raymondville, Texas, so many hours and miles away, I can't say. But I do know that the news came in over the switchboard. Even as isolated as we were in Raymondville, somebody must have had a relative on the West Coast, who had gotten the news from Hawaii, and who then called home.

My mother was working alone that Sunday, so she took the call. Because the operator who worked Sunday was paid time and a half, Mother had asked for those hours. When she came straight from work to pick me up before the party was actually over, I was alarmed when she appeared. I didn't want to go because I was having a good time. Thalia Gayle's mother had planned funny games with nice prizes. More to the point, we hadn't eaten our cake and ice cream.

Mother motioned to L. C., Thalia Gayle's father. They stood in the entryway and talked. Both of them looked worried to death. Helen went over and listened too. When she came back, she stopped the games almost immediately and served the refreshments.

Before Thalia Gayle had opened all her presents, other cars and pickups started pulling into the front yard. The men congregated beside the vehicles. Some were pacing. Some leaned braced against the doors and the fenders. One of them seemed to be punctuating his speech by kicking a tire on his pickup. We all could see them through the front windows and through the screen door.

They were smoking cigarettes, throwing the butts down, and grinding them out with their heels as if they wanted to drill a hole in the grass. Their talk grew louder and louder. Once in a while, we children would overhear a dirty word, but no one giggled. We were all uneasy, aware that something terrible had happened.

The women gathered in the kitchen. Someone started crying about her brother. He was supposed to be in San Diego, California, but he might be "over there"—wherever "there" was. I hardly noticed Thalia Gayle's gifts because I was listening so hard.

The December evening was already darkening. In the Valley darkness comes almost like a curtain dropping because of the absence of mountains and tall trees. The sun drops below the flat western horizon and even its rays are gone within minutes.

As if it were a signal, everyone took his child and left. The pickup trucks and Chevrolet and Ford sedans drove off down the lanes, their headlights cutting the countryside into squares. I huddled in my coat and watched them disappear.

Then Mother tried to explain what had happened.

"We've been attacked. America is at war. The Japanese have bombed Pearl Harbor in Hawaii. Do you know where Hawaii is, Mona Dean?"

I didn't know whether to shake my head or nod it. I didn't know where Hawaii was, or even what it was, but I had seen black silhouettes of bombers roaring through the sky and dropping bombs over countries far away. The Movietone News showed them every time I went to the movies. I also knew what Japanese children looked like, from a picture in my geography book. They didn't look like me.

"Where?" I asked.

"It's in the Pacific Ocean."

I remembered how to spell Pacific. Still I didn't have the least idea what she was talking about. I couldn't understand what was making my mother so very unhappy.

She reached over and patted me. "Don't worry about it," she said. "It won't ever come here. You'll be safe."

I crawled over against her and put my head in her lap. Until that minute I hadn't thought that I might not be. I doubled my fists up underneath my chin. It was one thing more to worry about.

We didn't have to wait very long to see what was going to happen.

Just before Christmas, Uncle Jack came to see us. The sight of him drove me into ecstasies of excitement. He was so beautiful in his forest green uniform with all the brass buttons. He'd joined the army. I was thrilled. I never thought about what terrible danger he might be going into.

His smile was fairly glowing. He was so happy. His older brothers Oslin and A. Y. had joined too. Of course, he wanted to be like them. Three Damron sons—at twenty-two he was the youngest—were all going into harm's way.

He certainly looked like the perfect soldier. Young, strong, fearless, a Texan born and bred. A farm boy with unquestioning patriotism, he was eager for the fight. The army scarcely had to train him. He could hit dead center anything within the range of his weapon. With a rifle against his shoulder, he could move silently through forty acres of *brasada* and drop a whitetail deer on the run or a wild turkey on the wing.

Mammaw picked up Allen, who wasn't even three yet, and held him so tightly he squeaked. Her face was grave. I felt cold all over as a glimmer of what might happen to him dawned in my brain.

I could believe with my whole heart that "Uncle Sam needed him." At the same time I started to weep. I was afraid he'd be shot.

He flashed his glorious warm smile. He held Allen and me and promised to send us postcards. He waved as he drove away.

The truth was that he never saw action. I overheard Aunt Jane say in a bitter voice that he fought the battle of Matagorda Bay. Later I learned that's where the stockade was. Whether he was inside or outside I never knew. Nor did I know why he wasn't in Europe or the Pacific.

Perhaps the rebellious, independent streak in his makeup made him too undisciplined to follow orders without question. But he was certainly courageous. The army missed a great ranger or a leader for a reconnaissance patrol.

He'll always be a hero to me. After all, I saw him come to our backdoor with his smile in place despite a rattlesnake bite.

$$\pi\pi\pi$$

The War Effort came to Robert E. Lee Elementary School in little ways. We were little children in a little town in a little county in the southernmost tip of Texas. But so pervasive was the anger generated by the sneak attack on Pearl Harbor that every child wanted to help kick Hirohito and Hitler in the seat of the pants as portrayed in cartoons. We might be little, but we were fierce.

After the Pledge of Allegiance to the flag displayed on a pole beside the blackboard, we would copy patriotic songs into our songbooks. When we finished copying each song, our teacher Miss Juanita Pollard would teach us to sing it *a cappella.*

Eyes fastened on the flag, heads high, little chests swelled with pride and patriotism, hearts throbbing to a martial beat, we belted out "God Bless America." We learned and sang "America the Beautiful." Miss Pollard told us to bow our heads when we sang the last verse of "My Country 'Tis of Thee."

Our fathers' God to Thee,
Author of Liberty,
To Thee we sing;
Long may our land be bright
With freedom's holy light,
Protect us by Thy might,
Great God, our King.

We'd go crazy singing "Yankee Doodle" because we got to march around the room. Then we'd stand at attention again for all four verses of the "Star-Spangled Banner."

To be closer to our fathers and brothers, we learned "Anchors Aweigh," "When Those Caissons Go Rolling Along," "*Semper Paratus,*" "The Marine's Hymn," and "Off We Go into the Wild Blue Yonder." The boys particularly liked that one because they could play at firing machine guns when we sang about "...down we dive spouting our flames from under...."

We must have been something to hear and see.

Posters, radio, newsreels all reminded us that every single thing we saved would help us win the war and save a soldier's life. We were told to write on both front and back of the paper, so as not to waste a sheet. When we had finished an exercise and it had been graded and recorded in Miss Pollard's grade book, we passed it to the front. Then the row monitors would put it in the big box that held our scrap paper contributions.

I heard my mother say they had started printing paperback books. They were made to conserve paper and to make them lighter to mail to the soldiers and sailors overseas, but she was glad for herself because she couldn't afford more than a quarter for a book.

Almost everybody wore dresses and shirts with red, white, and blue colors. One of the girls had a dress with a sailor collar with stars in the corners and around the hem.

We knew that "Loose lips sink ships," and what a sky pilot was. We knew virtually nothing about Hitler, Mussolini, and Hirohito except their names and what they looked like. Hitler, of course, had a black moustache and wore his hair slicked down over his forehead in a messy way. Our mothers would never let us go to school with hair in our face like that. Mussolini had a huge unshaven jaw and a funny cap with a tassel. Hirohito wore glasses and rode a white horse.

Those of us who were artistic like Emma Jean Clay could draw caricatures of them and then deface them very satisfactorily. I personally attempted to draw swastikas, so I could put inkblots all over them the way Byrne James did. Alas, I could never get all the bends off the arms of the crosses to go in the right directions. As a fourth grader, art was my worst subject. Mammaw had never encouraged me to draw freehand.

Miss Pollard handed out cards with airplane silhouettes on them. If a Zero or a Messerschmitt, Mitsubishi or Junker Ju flew over, we could tell our parents, and they could tell the Air Raid Warden to blow the siren. Since my mother was a telephone operator, she blew the siren everyday at noon. Since she was right there, so to speak, I volunteered to report directly to my mother if anyone wanted to tell me. That way we could warn everybody quicker.

I thought several boys, including Byrne James, looked at me enviously.

More cards showed silhouettes of Lockheed Lightnings, Curtiss Helldivers, Liberator Bombers, and Flying Fortresses, so we wouldn't make mistakes. We were also given pictures of British Spitfires and Hawker Hurricanes to be on the safe side. Of course, all the boys were in love with the names of the planes and rat-a-tat-tatted from the seesaws and giant strides at recess.

I was in the thick of it, saving paper like mad, memorizing plane silhouettes, singing lustily. But there was one thing that I couldn't do.

I wasn't able to buy Defense Stamps.

On Fridays we were allowed to buy these pink postage stamp size pictures of the Minute Man in his tricorne hat stepping over his plow with his musket in his hand. They cost ten cents apiece.

We would paste them in our stamp books; and when we got $18.50 worth, we could turn them in and get a $25.00 bond. I was passionate to have one. It occurred to me that with only thirty-four weeks in the school year, it would take five and half years to get that bond. I simply had to buy more stamps. I begged Mother for more money. At eight years of age in the fourth grade, I couldn't earn money for myself.

We were so poor that ten cents was a lot of money. Mother couldn't afford more than a dime a week. She explained to me that she had to buy gasoline at ten cents a gallon for the old car, some groceries although we grew most of our food, and shoes for me at fifty cents a pair.

She also told me that she had written to my father, who was in the army just like Uncle Jack, even though he had a "rheumatic heart." Evidently the draft board didn't believe him any more than Mammaw did. The purpose of her letter had been to ask him to make out an allotment for me the way Jack had for Allen. My father had never answered back. He didn't care to give even a small amount of his pay for his daughter's care even though the army would have matched it dollar for dollar.

I thought about him every Friday for a while. If he'd sent me an allotment, I could have used it to buy defense stamps so he would be safer. He was missing a chance to save his own life. I came to decide that he wasn't very smart.

I watched dismally as other children brought in quarters and half dollars, sometimes even whole dollars. No doubt their fathers fished them from their pockets without a thought.

Moreover, we were having a contest with the other fourth grade to see who could buy the most stamps and bonds. Since we were the high fourth and they were the low, we had to win. When I would bring in only ten cents every week, I was sure that everyone looked down on me. I was embarrassed and sad because I wasn't "doing my part." In a real way I was glad when school let out in May. I didn't have to feel bad every Friday.

The next year things were different. The soldiers and sailors were winning, and we didn't buy defense stamps any more.

As a matter of record, my mother sounded the siren only once during the whole of World War II. She blew it in the middle of a spring afternoon shortly after I came home from school. The sun was shining in a bright blue sky.

A few minutes later she called Mammaw. The news had just reached Raymondville that President Franklin Delano Roosevelt had died. I think that was the first time I saw my grandmother burst into tears.

ππππ

On our bi-monthly excursions to the library in Harlingen, Mammaw couldn't help but notice that the road was lined with soldiers and sailors hitchhiking to and from the bases in Brownsville and Harlingen. For many days we drove right on by.

I was pretty sure she didn't stop and pick them up because she was ashamed of our dilapidated old rattletrap of a car.

I didn't know that she thought giving a ride might not be ladylike. She was a fifty-six-year-old woman with an eight-year-old girl and a four-year-old boy in an old blue Chevrolet sedan with two doors. With no man driving, she didn't know what the service men would think.

Until the day it rained. Not just a light, drifting warm rain, but a cloudburst with thunder and lightning. And a pair of boys in blue bell-bottom trousers standing like drowned puppies by the roadside.

Mammaw's tender heart couldn't leave them. She put on the brake and nodded to me. I opened the door.

Apologizing for being so wet, they immediately pulled off their white caps and crawled into the backseat. Allen was delighted as was I. He always rode back there alone standing on the hump formed by the drive shaft. Now two grown men about the same age as his father shared the space with him. The very fact that he was close to two adults of his own sex was a thrill for him. Probably for the first time, he actually sat down on the seat between them and tried to look older and taller.

The boys introduced themselves to Mammaw. They told her where they came from and that they were going to Brownsville. They were extremely polite. I told them where we were going and why. They smiled and nodded.

They were impressive. Spotlessly clean, sporting fresh haircuts and shaves. They said "Yes, Ma'am," to Mammaw. When she let them out under the canopy at the Sinclair station, they said, "Thank you, Ma'am, and much obliged."

Allen looked like he wanted to go with them. He climbed up in the seat and looked through the back window to wave as we pulled away.

Wheels began to turn in my grandmother's mind. They had accepted the ride she offered and not said anything but thanks. They had been grateful for what she did. At last! At last! She had found a way to aid in the War Effort. She could give the boys rides.

As we started back to Raymondville, she stopped for three more. The backseat was full. Again the boys were on their best behavior. We were all delighted.

I greeted Mother at the door with the news. "We gave some soldiers rides," I bubbled. "It was raining and we kept them from getting wet. They were from Pennsylvania and Georgia."

Mother looked at Mammaw. "Mother! You didn't pick up hitchhikers?"

"Oh, no," I said instantly. "They were sailors and on the way back we picked up soldiers."

"Mother!"

Mammaw folded her arms. "They needed rides. Everybody should do it."

When Mammaw folded her arms, she meant business.

Mother looked at me. "Are you teaching her to do something dangerous?"

I couldn't figure out why it was dangerous. The boys were so nice. But I held my breath.

Mammaw shook her head. "It's for the War Effort," she said. And then she added, "I can't do anything else."

For two years my grandmother picked up hitchhiking sailors and soldiers, carried them twenty miles on their journeys and let them out with "Good luck and Godspeed."

Sometimes we had as many as five in the old car. Four would crowd into the backseat and one sat in the front. He had to hold Allen in his lap while I sat against Mammaw's side and held her purse.

We never had a thought that we were not perfectly safe. None of us in that time could conceive that they might rob her of the few dollars and change she carried, strip her of her gold wedding band, and the little gold hoops in her ears, steal the old Chevrolet, or do something dreadful to us.

We never gave a thought to danger.

They were our fathers, our sons, and our brothers, as President Franklin Delano Roosevelt told us over and over on the Movietone News. If Mammaw had had car trouble, I have no doubt they would have piled out and fixed her flat tire, or rolled the car to a service station.

Mammaw said whenever she picked up a soldier she thought of Uncle Jack and and his brother Oslin. Whenever, she picked up an airman, she thought of Uncle Jack's brother A. Y., whom we learned much later became a fighter pilot ace. Most especially Mammaw thought of her nephew George E. Lusk, somewhere in Europe. Whenever she picked up a sailor she thought of his brother Charles Patton, her "Little Pat," on a ship somewhere in the Pacific.

Everyone she helped tugged at her heart. She was so proud that she had found a way to "do her part."

πππ

Aunt Jane was transferred from Harlingen to Corsicana. She badly wanted to spend some time with her son, so Mammaw took Allen and me there to spend the summer. Because we were more or less without friends in a strange city for three weeks, Mammaw devised an activity of us.

First, let me say that Mammaw had bad eyesight.

As a child she had had a terrible infection of some sort that manifested itself in sties on her eyelids. They had been extremely painful and her eyes had swelled almost shut. The doctor in Booneville in 1890 hadn't known anything to do but tell her mother to rub on some all-purpose grease. When the sties finally went away of their own accord and the infection subsided, her vision was impaired.

Consequently, she'd worn bifocals all her life while my mother and I had the eyes of eagles.

She didn't like to read because it strained her eyes and gave her headaches. Her capacity for love and sacrifice clearly manifests itself here. Although she read to me as often as I asked and drove Allen and me to the library twice a month, she never checked out a book for herself. She spent hours of time for a venture she herself didn't participate in.

On the other hand, she could crochet. She memorized the patterns and practiced them until she really didn't need to see except occasionally. Like the fingers of a fine pianist striking the proper keys, her fingers moved with magical precision using a six-inch silver hook to loop a single thread of cotton or silk into the next loop and the next and the next, in and about and through each other until she formed all sorts of fanciful designs.

Whenever I watched her, I was always amazed. Of course, I didn't watch her very often. And I strenuously resisted her efforts to teach me how to do it. I'd much rather play in the salt cedars.

At first she worked in bedspread cotton making heavy pieces in traditional pineapple, pinwheel, and hexagon patterns. But bedspread cotton thread came in white, cream, and ecru. The thread was coarse; the colors were bland. She made some beautiful heirloom pieces, but her ambitions were elsewhere.

She loved beautiful colors. She loved the feel of silk. So she began projects of such magnitude that I can only liken them to giant murals. Rembrandt, Picasso, and Rivera worked with giant blocks of color. My grandmother worked with thin silk thread. If the worth of art were deemed intrinsic as well as extrinsic then their products would be nothing compared to hers. She crocheted two bedspreads—one for Mother and one for Aunt Jane. They were identical because Allen and I helped her select the pieces once they were finished and string the tiny hexagons together.

Here is how we did it.

Everywhere we went during those terrible years of World War II, Mammaw bought balls of silk thread. Only small amounts of silk were available, so the task for Allen and me was to run to the notion counter of Woolworth's and find the new shades. Our quest was for dozens and dozens of different shades and variegations of the primary and secondary colors.

Then wherever we went, be it to the park, to my music lessons, to choir practice, to the library, Mammaw carried a ball of silk and a crochet hook. In less than a minute she could make a thumb-sized center made up of a tiny requisite chained circle and radiating from it a series of double crochets with chains at the corners. Then she'd make another, so she'd have two—for Mother and one for Aunt Jane.

When the requisite number of these centers was completed—surely numbering in the thousands. She began again crocheting an edge of double crochets and chains in another color. The process was done for the third time in white. Two of every combination separated into two bags and carefully stored.

When every piece was completed came the most wonderful task for Allen and me.

Mammaw spread a sheet on the floor and dumped all the little pieces from one bag onto it. She made us wash our grubby little hands just as she always did before she picked up whatever piece she was working on.

"Now," she said. "Let's arrange all the pieces as they'll go on your mother's bedspreads."

"Our mother's bedspreads?" Allen couldn't believe her. "Us?"

"So no two colors are close together," Mammaw said.

This task was a challenge, a joy, a sharing of creativity. We were helping our grandmother make something beautiful for our mothers. We were learning colors that no school could ever teach us—ocher, both raw and burnt umber, crimson and carmine and scarlet, emerald, jade, aquamarine, Nile, teal, sapphire, azure, robin's egg, buttercup, primrose, eggshell, sienna, maroon, puce, violet.

We worked for days. When one was finished, we had to start all over again and match all the blocks in the other, so the two bedspreads would be identical.

Then while she held two big carpet needles with a length of string on each, we pushed each one down over the blunt tip. Allen and I each picked up the identical hexagons and pushed them at the same time. We did this for each row and Mammaw labeled each one.

Our job was done, but we both watched her every step of the way as she crocheted them together. I wish I knew how many hours she spent. I wish I remembered how many years.

Both Allen and I treasure those bedspreads today. Whenever I use mine, I know I am using a work of art beyond price. My grandmother created it. At the same time she enabled her two grandchildren to be part of the work she created and to feast their eyes on hundreds of colors and shades of shining silk.

My grandmother's masterpieces are considered domestic art, the designation for utilitarian things. Although museums across the country are exhibiting these pieces, they still have not been given the recognition of fine art or "great art."

To my way of thinking, they are far superior. Perhaps great art inspires people with its magnitude. But in terms of conception and execution, my grandmother's silk bedspreads are an inspiration.

As far as their worth is concerned, I can think of nothing more worthy than the creation of beauty that lights a room and keeps a child warm on a cool spring evening.

πππ

In the middle of World War II came rationing. I suppose there was some reason to it, but to tell the truth, I can't think why. Rationing rubber. Yes. Because America couldn't grow of drill for any of it. The milky substance from which our tires was made came from plantations in Asian countries that had been overrun by the Japanese.

But why gasoline? Texas was sitting on a lake of oil. Why sugar? The bayous of Louisiana were full of sugar cane. Why butter? From Texas to Wisconsin thousands of head of cattle grazed. And why shoes? Those cattle all had hides, didn't they?

Since the war only lasted three and half years, most people were only slightly inconvenienced. They never really felt the *pinch*—a bit of humor there.

The truth was that I was often pinched. I was seven and eight and nine years old and growing at a phenomenal rate. Indeed, I grew out of my clothes within a few weeks. To keep my body decently covered, Mammaw could let down hems, set in belts, and make new dresses. She also cut off her own coats and slips and nightgowns. But she couldn't make shoes. And under no circumstances were my feet going to be neglected. One of her priorities was that I should have strong straight feet—no corns, bunions, nor crooked toes.

Aunt Jane and Mother had inflicted suffering on themselves when they were young because vanity had decreed that no lady had feet larger than the respectable Size 7. Too late they switched to Size 9's. Their toes were cramped and twisted.

So Mammaw swore that I wouldn't wear shoes too short for me. She gave me her ration stamps. Mother gave me hers. We sneaked in the back door of Abraham Rios Boots in Raymondville. For fifty cents a pair, he sold sandals made from scraps of colored hide. They were really delightful little shoes. One month my shoes were sky blue and white. The next month they were Cordovan red and tan.

Mr. Rios would set me down, put my foot on piece of tablet paper, and trace around it with a pencil. The next day I'd have a new pair of shoes. They were just leather strips sewn on a flat sole with a quarter inch of bull-hide for a heel. But they kept my feet off the ground. But winter came on. I couldn't wear barefoot sandals in December. Even though the Valley was warm, it wasn't that warm.

The other children in my classes seemed to have no problems probably because we were all wearing hand-me-downs. Only the oldest boy and girl got new shoes. And they got all their brothers' and sisters' ration stamps.

That's where I ran into trouble. I didn't have any sisters. So Mother asked around. Where could she get new shoes for me? Finally, Jesse Starck, a friend of hers with a more daring streak, told her.

Mexico!

It was only fifty miles away to Matamoros. The largest city on either side of the Rio Grande, was a thriving metropolis in the northernmost part of the state of Tamaulipas. Mother was uncertain. She had heard all sorts of stories about that place.

There were houses "of ill repute" south of the river. One reason Mother was so uncomfortable with Mammaw's picking up service men going and coming was that she was sure that for many of them the ultimate destination was the bars and baudy houses on the Mexican side. We also heard stories about how perfectly healthy young men would cross the border and simply disappear, never to be seen again. Surely, they couldn't be hiding out in Mexico to avoid going into the army.

Moreover, everyone knew about Mexican bandits. Everyone remembered old man Meade. And more recently, stories were circulating at the telephone office—whose girls heard everything—that bandits armed with German rifles had crossed the river, driven north, and raided the Norias section of the King Ranch. A special group of men called the Norias Rangers had fought them off and driven them back across the river.

In those days Americans could go across the border with a wave of the hand to the Mexican border guards. On the way back the American border patrol stopped people to find out if they were all American citizens and whether or not they had any plants or fruits.

My mother didn't want to make the trip. But she looked at my toes lapping over the tips of my last pair of barefoot sandals. We were halfway through December. She was desperate. She discussed the expedition with Mammaw.

Mammaw was always game. It was worth a try. Holding our breaths, Mother, Mammaw, Allen, and I drove across the rickety bridge stretched above the muddy Rio Grande. For the first time I saw the Big River from which the Valley got its name. Beneath us flashed surging brown water between high clay banks thickly grown with little mesquite trees and green reeds.

We crossed into a foreign country, where people didn't even speak English.

And none of us spoke a word of Spanish.

Following directions supplied by Jesse, Mother drove down the dusty street toward the market. The sidewalks were only a couple of feet wide. The buildings had no windows opening onto the street. Their walls rose on either side of us. We might have been driving through a bleached adobe canyon. Up ahead we saw a church spire, quite the tallest church spire I'd ever seen.

A bony horse drawing a rickety two-wheeled cart pulled out in front of us. The driver was perched on a load of cantaloupes.

Mother shifted down into second, and we crept along behind him. There wasn't room to pass even if Mother had dared to. She was determined to draw no undue attention to herself.

Fine yellow dust fell away from the cart's ironbound wheels. The south side of the Rio Grande has a very different geography from the north side. The Valley in the United States is the river delta. Its alluvial soil is washed from the land the river travels through. The Mexican side is the riverbank, the edge of the dry northeastern slopes of the Sierra Madre Oriental.

Life is much poorer because the people have fewer resources. I was a farmer's granddaughter. I lived on a rich and prosperous farm. Even without a geography lesson, I knew what made the difference. I could tell by the dust.

It wasn't the rich brown of our farm. It was light yellowish tan. The children playing in the dust alongside the street were dusty. When I played hard in my yard, I got dirty. I could recognize the difference. Arid yellow dust covered their skin and lightened their black hair. My good black dirt would cake on my knees and rear. I wondered how well tomatoes would grow in such clayey soil. It seemed too fine to hold moisture.

As all these idle thoughts were flitting through me head, we arrived at El Mercado. From the very first glance, all of us knew it wasn't Brenner's Grocery Store.

The first things I noticed were the skinned carcasses of goats hanging from a pole. As they swung in the breeze, flies buzzed around them.

I wrinkled my nose as I stared and stared. Then I looked at Mammaw to see what she thought about them. She had her hand over her mouth. Her eyes were fixed straight ahead. She wasn't sick at her stomach; she was appalled.

We parked the car and instantly dusty little boys besieged us. "Watch your car, *Senora*?" they offered. "Only a nickel."

My mother looked astounded, but she nodded at the cleanest ones. "You two," she said. "Watch my car."

Another one tried to sell me a tiny package of Chiclets gum. I didn't know what to say, but I was probably fortunate not to have had any money. Mammaw's expression was stern as she shook her head. She would have died under torture before I could have put a piece of that gum in my mouth.

Mother took my hand more tightly than usual. Mammaw took Allen's. He was barely four and fascinated by it all. He loved to play with boys, but Mammaw's grip meant business. Besides he was a little frightened by so many little dusty, ragged barefoot boys all chattering in a language he couldn't understood one word of. He hung close to her skirt.

We walked in under the maze of awnings that was the Matamoros Mercado. On every side were things I'd never seen before. One vendor had an enormous selection of shiny clay pots with Mexican and Indian designs painted in bright colors. They were all sizes including tea sets for dolls with cups and saucers no bigger than the tip of a finger. The vendor held one out in the palm of his hand.

"You want, *niñita*? How much your mother give me?"

I wanted to look more closely, but Mother dragged me right on by.

Another man had a selection of knives and whips. Allen almost pulled Mammaw's arm off. Fortunately, before he could pitch a fit, he was distracted when a man walked by carrying a huge swaying tower of crêpe paper *piñatas* on a pole.

One stand had wool coats like the turquoise one Ona Lou Savage wore to school. I really wanted one, but they were two dollars. I didn't ask because I knew that wasn't what we came for.

Everywhere vendors were calling to us to buy. Mammaw and Mother were getting more nervous and frustrated. Allen and I were so excited we were dancing up and down like puppies on leashes.

Then two bright-eyed boys presented themselves to us by bowing formally from the waist, right arms crooked across their stomachs, left arms across their backs. They wore white cotton dress shirts and polished shoes. Their hair was neatly combed. They spoke formal English with only a trace of any accent.

"What do you want, *Señora*?" the taller one asked carefully. He looked to be my age. His companion was younger. Were they really six and eight? They looked so grown up.

Mother consulted a piece of paper. *"Z-zapatos,"* she stammered. She pushed me forward. "For her."

The taller one looked up into my face and down at my feet. He shook his head faintly at their size. I shuffled them miserably. His hands and feet were small. Then he smiled a bright white-toothed smile. "You come this way."

He bowed to my mother. His brother bowed to my grandmother. He led the way and his brother brought up the rear. They did it so deftly and politely that we thought we were being escorted. We didn't realize we'd been captured and were being brought in like strays.

I didn't know that those boys were already working for their father and uncle. They were the Pizaña brothers, and at six and eight they were already entrepreneurs.

I bought my shoes from them. And came back the next month and bought some more. Over the years we've grown up together. I always go to them first for anything that I want in Mexico. Mother bought my luggage—a four-piece matched set—all leather—to go to college. I've bought fine pieces of sterling silver jewelry and beautiful leather purses. I've bought linens and lace.

When the time came for me to marry, instead of patronizing a bridal shop in Dallas, I went to the brothers Pizaña, who were settling into manhood with fine moustaches and gold wedding rings of their own. From them I purchased French illusion for my veil, heavy slipper satin for my petticoat, and exquisite *peau de soie* embroidered with lilies of the valley for my wedding dress.

They congratulated me and smiled as happily as if I were their own *hermana*. When my daughter was born, they were sincerely happy for me. When my grandmother and later my mother died, they were sincerely sorry.

For a long time I've hugged the brothers when I visit their stands. Once in a while I'll catch sight of a flock of tourists staring at me as I embrace grown men in the midst of the market hubbub.

I always smile and wiggle my fingers at them. After all, I've known the Pizañas longer than I've known almost everyone else except members of my own family—more than half a century. They're some of my oldest friends.

$$\pi\pi\pi$$

I never learned to milk a cow. I know Mammaw let me try the one or two times that I asked, but I never got the hang of it. I couldn't grasp strongly enough with my fingers. And to tell the truth, I didn't much want to learn. On top of a horse was wonderful. Under a cow was *not*.

Mammaw never seemed to mind sitting down on a stool beside a brindle belly with its huge pink udder veined and swollen till it looked about to burst. While the cow contentedly chewed her cud, Mammaw would wash the teats with warm water and slip the milk pail beneath. Effortlessly she'd squeeze and strip, and the warm milk would squirt into the pail. As the pail filled, its contents would foam and froth. All the cats would sit around in a circle and watch with bright eyes, occasionally mewing piteously as if they couldn't wait a minute longer.

This scene repeated over and over twice daily strikes me now with its unreality. The fact that most of the people alive today have never touched a cow let alone its udder speaks of the passage of time more eloquently than anything else that I know. How can we Americans who live with milk, butter, cheese, ice cream, and yogurt be so far removed from its simple source?

Not that anyone who knew about it would want to return to the source.

The milk cows that I remember were disgusting creatures. From the slimy, liquid-soap feel of the huge bulbous nose to the unraveling rope at the end of a long floppy tail, a cow is a mistake of nature.

Even at a walk everything about them is ungainly, ungraceful, bobbing and flopping. At a wallowing lope—the highest speed of which they are capable—they look as if they'll fly apart at any minute. The hind legs swing out in opposite directions because they have to clear around the huge bulging udder with its dangling teats. The front legs with their great cloven hooves have to negotiate around the dewlap as it flops under their necks. It's not a pretty sight.

Cows do not moo or low gently very often. Mostly they bawl. When a cow bawls, the entire beast swells and extends. The trumpeting, growling bass bray makes a jackass sound pleasant. What flops out when they lift their tails aside is one of the great messes of the animal kingdom. Pollution on a grand scale.

Moreover, cows are a murderous combination of stupidity and treachery. Many a black and white Holstein has slashed a sharp-tipped curving horn into the thigh or knee of an unwary farmer who didn't get the feed out quickly enough. Many a Guernsey has suddenly kicked pail, stool, and milkmaid head over tin-cups.

One night Ole Blue, a big black-faced Guernsey with a dark steel-blue cast to her brindle hide was feeling vicious. She wouldn't allow another cow to drink before her at the water tank. More than once she'd tried to hook me as I leaned over it or merely stood beside it.

Mammaw was out milking after dark in December. Mother and I were in the house getting supper when we heard Ole Blue's cowbell set up a frantic clanking. Mother went to the back porch. It was already pitch black outside.

"Mother!" my mother called.

No one answered.

"Mother!" she shouted.

She plunged off the porch and ran into the darkness. I had never seen her leap like that.

"Mother!" I heard her scream again.

I was paralyzed. Suddenly, I wasn't brave at all. Instead I began to shiver. I don't think I'd ever been so afraid. What had happened out there in the dark was terrifying me. I was so afraid that something had happened to my grandmother. How could I live without her?

I heard more cowbells clanking again. I heard my mother yelling. Still I stood there. All my imagined courage and daring had deserted me in the face of real danger.

At last out of the darkness came my mother and grandmother. My grandmother was walking by herself. She looked all right.

But she was hurt. When she came into the light, I saw she was bleeding. I started to cry. I knew how I hurt when I bled.

My mother made Mammaw sit down in a kitchen chair. She took a basin of hot water and washed the whole of Mammaw's right arm and leg.

"What happened?" I managed to ask.

"Ole Blue jerked Mother down and dragged her." My mother's voice shook with anger.

My grandmother's injured side and arm were very weak and tender even after ten years. Because the doctors at Fort Smith had scraped her from spine to sternum and armpit to waist during her radical mastectomy, only skin remained to cover Mammaw's ribs on her right side. Both it and her shoulder were badly bruised. The outside of her arm was scraped, as well as the underside. Her knee was swelling beneath a wide abrasion that extended halfway up her thigh. Her blood ran all the way down into her shoe.

I watched shivering uncontrollably with tears trickling down my cheeks. Was Mammaw going to die?

Of course, she didn't. The bleeding was already stopping. Mother made Mammaw eat a bite of supper and then put her to bed.

Mammaw got up the next morning as usual although she hobbled badly for several days. The scabs on her leg and arm were enormous and the swelling didn't go down in her knee for weeks. The incident wasn't discussed in my presence ever again.

I focused my vengeful anger on Ole Blue and from her to all of her ilk. I lobbed clods of dirt at her flanks when she led the herd from the pasture to the tank. She jumped and tossed her head, but I didn't do her nearly enough damage.

She was ugly, nasty, treacherous, and stupid, stupid, stupid.

To this day I despise cows.

The worst was yet to come.

Quite by chance, I overheard Mother tell Aunt Jane, "The old cow dragged Mother last month. That's it. I'm not going to stay out here any longer. Maybe I'll get a "B" ration card and maybe I won't. They say telephone operators are essential. But they may change their minds.

"Anyway, I'll use that excuse to Mother. We're going to move into town. Our mother isn't going to stay out here and work like a field hand until it kills her."

Within a very short time Mother had made a down payment on a house in town just three blocks from the telephone office. It was a bigger, nicer house than she would have been able to afford under ordinary circumstances. In this case, someone else's tragedy was our good luck. The former owner Mrs. Decker had been electrocuted as she pulled vines down from the outside walls. Most people didn't feel comfortable about buying a house a person had died in. It just might be haunted. People told each other ghost stories that they swore were true.

I began to be excited about the move. I could walk to school rather than ride the school bus. I would have friends to play with. I might see a ghost.

I didn't realize what I was leaving, didn't recognize what I'd lost until I lost it. I lost the way of life that I loved. I lost the security of being in the center of hundreds of acres of my own land.

Although I was still a child, I was forced to close the door on the unique parts of my childhood. I would never have them again.

I lost the freedom of farm.

I lost the salt cedars.

ππππ

My Aunt Jane moved very quickly from Franklin's Stores in Corsicana to San Antonio. There she managed the Parisian, the upscale end of the Franklin's corporation. It stocked much better clothing. All the salesladies had to wear black dresses and high heels and hose.

I'm sure Mammaw hated to have her younger daughter more or less permanently far away. Our family, as much as any other, reflected the breaking apart of close-knit American families everywhere. Allen stayed with us in Raymondville. When Aunt Jane came to visit him every few weekends, we'd all drive twenty miles west to San Manuel to meet the bus from San Antonio.

The switchboard at the telephone company remained open all night for the soldiers to call home from the East Coast and West Coast and sometimes from overseas. Mother started working nights because those hours paid double-time.

When Christmas, 1943, came, we had a problem. How could we get the family together in one spot for Christmas Eve and Christmas Day? Mother had to work all night Christmas Eve. Aunt Jane couldn't leave San Antonio until Christmas Day. Then she might not get a seat on the bus because it might be full of service men trying to get home to their families.

So began the tradition that carried us through the darkest days of the war. Santa Claus ceased to come to our house at his usual time.

Mother and Mammaw set Allen and me down and explained the problem to us. Aunt Jane had to stay in San Antonio and keep the store open for the soldiers and sailors to buy gifts for their mothers, sisters, sweethearts, and wives. Mother had to work all night, to keep the phone lines open for the soldiers to call home.

"But Santa Claus doesn't work in San Antonio or at the phone company," I was quick to point out.

"But he's even busier than salesladies or telephone operators," Mother said.

I'd seen my mother working at the switchboard with her headset on her head, opening those keys, picking up the plugs, punching them in the holes that made the connections, ringing the telephone bells, pulling the plugs out when the lights went off indicating that people had finished talking and hung up.

I felt sorry for Santa Claus if he was busier than a telephone operator.

Mammaw went on to say that having Christmas all together on December 24th or 25th was impossible. But we'd still have it and it would be even better. She made everything seem right.

Of course, we understood that the soldiers and sailors in uniform had to have their presents delivered on time. They couldn't be disappointed so far away from their home and families.

So Santa Claus would visit us on a different schedule when we were least expecting him. I don't remember when he came that year, but he did come.

And for all our years and years, he always came at special times, long after we knew in our minds although not in our hearts that he didn't exist. Long after the soldiers came home although some never came home. Long after most families could be together at Christmas time, he came at special times for us because he understood that our mothers had to work.

We might come home from school at four o'clock on the last day before the holidays to find Christmas dinner cooking, the strings of electric lights shining bright on the tree, and gaily wrapped packages stacked beneath it. He'd been and gone.

We might be called out of bed at six o'clock on December 21st to find he'd already left. We might learn that he couldn't make it until December 26th.

But we knew he'd never fail us.

And that has made all the difference in our lives.

πππ

The year after the war was over, Uncle Jack came home. He learned that his son's grandmother had been teaching Allen how to shoot. With a twinge of guilt, he came round with a .22 rifle and took Allen off somewhere to teach him to shoot it. He didn't give Allen the gun, but he promised to come around regularly and take Allen hunting.

Of course, he never did. He would call and set a date. Allen would sit on the front porch watching the road, at first eagerly, then with gradually dawning unhappiness, then finally in miserable exhaustion.

Surely, Jack Damron in his fecklessness never had any idea of the misery he created.

Mammaw would bring Allen in for supper and tell him that his father had probably gotten busy at some job.

I wasn't fooled by her explanation. I thought about my own father whom I hadn't seen since Mother brought me to the Valley. I didn't even remember what he looked like. Mother had taken his picture down when we'd moved from the farm and never bothered to put it up again. He'd promised he'd come to see me too, but he never had.

I didn't say anything to Allen about that. Allen was little and I loved him. Eventually, he came not to expect anything from his father and that was good because Jack never brought gifts of any sort. I remember vividly one time on the day before Christmas, he came to our house to say hello. When he saw the tree all decorated, he didn't say a word. But when he got ready to leave he did something that only I saw. He pulled a handful of change out of his pocket. He sorted through it and selected a nickel and four pennies. He had a quarter, but he put it back in his pocket.

Merry Christmas for his son: Nine cents.

Yet Jack could never leave us alone.

For years he came and went in and out of our lives. We were always his family—much more so than his own parents and brothers. I think he really loved Mammaw and, of course, Allen and me.

He'd stop by the house every so often and visit with Allen. He'd greet us with us same brilliant smile and exaggerated compliments. We'd greet him with cheers of delight make a great fuss over him. He'd talk very seriously to Mammaw. She always treated him cordially.

And until his dying day, Jack drove around the farm, looking at it, checking on its crops, reporting to anyone who'd listen how he thought it looked, how he wouldn't have done such-and-such, how this-and-so would have made a better yield.

Call me cynical, but I think he regretted its loss most of all.

IX
Requiem

My life in the Valley, the idyllic life that I have depicted here, ended for a long, long space of years. I was sixteen when I graduated from high school and twenty when I graduated from college. My formal education complete, I lived and worked mostly in Dallas for over forty years. During that time I married Jim Sizer, the love of my life.

It is for Rachel our daughter that this book is intended. When she was born, my mother, of course, came immediately to visit bringing Mammaw with her. My grandmother was seventy-nine. Her health had not been good the summer that I was pregnant. I had spent most of that time with her.

When they drove back home, Mammaw grew weaker and weaker. Finally, Mother had to take her to the hospital. On New Years' Eve, I got the call to fly home to Raymondville. Rachel was six weeks old.

Of course, to bring such a tiny baby into a hospital, even the little, relatively primitive one in Raymondville, was unthinkable. But Mammaw had to see the baby. She had to see her first great-grandchild again.

The next afternoon, Dr. Baden gave Mammaw a shot that roused her from her semi-coma.

I hurried into the hospital to Mammaw's room. I opened the window while Mother stood outside the screen holding Rachel in her little pink dress, her pink-and-white striped sweater and matching booties.

I rolled Mammaw's bed to the window and cranked it up so my grandmother could see out. The four of us females, four generations of women joined by love, three of us the beloved fruits of the body of the one before, were close together. The January wind was sharp.

Mammaw gazed at her great granddaughter with such love... And I truly believed that Rachel gazed at her. Then Mammaw sighed and waved. "Take her out of the wind," she murmured softly. "Don't let her catch a cold."

"I'll bring her back tomorrow," I promised.

"Just love her," my grandmother said. "Just love her."

Then she relaxed back on the bed. I rolled it back into position, pulled the window down, and kissed her. "I'll take her home and get her situated. Then I'll be right back," I promised.

Her eyes had already closed. "Just love her."

ππ π

My grandmother died at seventy-nine just two and a half months after Rachel was born. She had held her great granddaughter in her arms and saw her line extended for another generation.

Allen and I and, of course, her daughters were left bereft. She had been the touchstone, the stabilizing influence, for all our lives. When our mothers died ten years later so very young, so unexpectedly within months of each other, we began to look to our own mortality.

Still, we had Jack if only for a very short time.

He collapsed and died on Sunday morning, February 23, 1997. He was seventy-eight, the last of his generation. His brothers had gone on long before him. I felt the wrench around my heart as surely as if he had been my father as well.

I'm sure that even as his eyes closed, his smile flickered.

The angels braced themselves for the advent of a different one of their kind. I can see him now. He smiled and winked and asked to borrow a harp. He sang "El Rancho Grande" and "Strawberry Roan," and they welcomed him into their fold with open wings.

God gave him that flashing smile and that glorious voice. Now God has it to enjoy just as He has the women who loved Him.

ππ π

My beloved salt cedars are gone. Even trees die standing in the course of eighty years. The picture on the cover of this book is of a windbreak several miles farther east.

The three houses that were originally built on the farm have long been moved away as well as all the barns and outbuildings. The windmill was blown over in a hurricane and never replaced. The tank that held water for the surroundings farms is the only vestige of what was a lovely, prosperous family farm.

But be at ease, Rachel Andrea. Secure in my heart and instilled in yours, my daughter, is the knowledge that if you should ever need a place to live, you can build again on your own land. And plant a windbreak.

Salt cedars grow very fast...

"That's what Mr. Roosevelt did for me. Don't you ever come back here and ask me to vote for Wendell Wilkie."

Without another word the man stuck his paper in his pocket and left.

Nowhere in the annals of American history is there a more telling explanation of why Roosevelt was elected for a third term.

ππ

Boys flying kites pull in their white-winged birds,
But you can't do that when you're flying words.
Careful with fire is good advice we know,
But careful with words is ten times doubly so.
Thoughts unexpressed may sometimes fall back dead
But God Himself can't stop them once they're said.

If my mother quoted this poem to me once, she quoted it a hundred times. I heard it so often that I could write it without pausing even though it's been at least forty years since last I heard it.

I should think before I spoke. I should keep my often-too-pointed observations to myself, for God Himself couldn't stop them once I'd said them.

Once we went shopping in Brasher & Jones, one of the better stores in the Valley. Since I didn't have any friends except Ruth, who didn't have any more money than I did, I didn't really want anything. Being reared on a dirt farm in the middle of nowhere left me with nothing to measure my lot in life against. I literally didn't know what to want.

Unfortunately, I was a wild thing—given to temper tantrums if I couldn't get my way despite Mammaw's best efforts.

Mother never knew what to expect, so she thought she'd best explain everything to me before we got in the store and I pitched a fit because I couldn't have something I wanted.

So she had told me, "Don't ask for anything in here, Mona Dean. Remember. We don't have any money."

I nodded in agreement. I knew we were poor. I understood we were going to look at dresses to see the styles, and then we would look at the materials to make the dresses to see what colors were going to be popular.

Then we would buy Butterick Patterns for twenty-five cents each and Mammaw would make the clothes out of materials we had at home. Incidentally, Mammaw and Mother were always trying to get me to sew, but I was too impatient to sit still for more than five minutes at a time. I had more important things to do in the salt cedars.

foot cords. The kitchen, the living room, the two bedrooms, and the sleeping porch all had lights. Brass beaded chains dangled from them, with strings attached to extend the chain another foot. Mammaw tied a button on the end of each string, so she could make a swipe with her hand and find the string in the middle of the night.

Suddenly, she could see at night to read to me. She could crochet. She could plug in the radio she'd brought from Arkansas. She could use her washing machine. She could use her electric iron. She could have hot water from a pipe, not from kettles that spilled and splashed and scalded skin.

No one alive today can imagine my grandmother's quiet joy. I can only guess at what she must have felt. I can only try to imagine what she must have thought. What praises and paeans she must have sung to God and to Franklin Delano Roosevelt.

How do I know?

One incident remains forever in my memory—the defining tale.

One day a man came to the backdoor. Everyone came to the backdoor.

He stood on the sleeping porch in front of my little grandmother and gave a rousing speech for the Republican Candidate Wendell Wilkie.

Mammaw stood with her arms folded tightly across her chest, her lips tight-closed and thin, her head cocked slightly to the side. Her eyes behind her gold-rimmed glasses were steely. I huddled against the doorframe. Mammaw looked like she was going to scold him.

When he finished, he tried to give her a piece of paper to help her to remember to vote for Wilkie. My grandmother wouldn't take it. As she waved it aside, she motioned him to follow her.

Into the kitchen she marched. Because the room was so small, we had no kitchen table. Instead a pantry of four shelves was hung on the wall. The door to that pantry opened at the top and let down. At the same time a single leg swung out to support it. It made a three-sided table that we ate around.

On one side of it was an enamel washbasin of rolled clothes that had been starched and thoroughly sprinkled, so they could be ironed. On the other side were stacks of finished ironing—sheets and pillowcases, play dresses, housedresses, handkerchiefs, a sunbonnet—all neatly folded.

At the end of the table, the ironing board was set up with the ironing cord running upward to the light. A two-way socket had been screwed in. One held the light bulb tilted out at a right angle. The other held a plug socket for the iron.

Everything looked perfectly normal—not unusual, not momentous. Then Mammaw pointed to the light bulb burning brightly.

"You see that," she said.

The man nodded, clearly puzzled.

concert halls. He became from a sissy the farthest thing that anyone could imagine.

He loved women and they loved him because he performed all the little courtesies without affectation. The only drawback was that he had problems throughout his life keeping a wife.

I believe I know why. He couldn't ever find anyone to compete with the care and adoration he received from his "Mammaw," his "Auntie Momma," and his "Sister."

ππππ

President Franklin Delano Roosevelt was elected in 1932 and 1936. In 1939 he ran again for an unprecedented third term.

Many people thought that he shouldn't do so. His own Vice-President John Nance Garner from Uvalde, Texas, quit as his running mate. Republicans everywhere vilified him and mounted a strong campaign against him with Wendell Wilkie as their candidate.

Mammaw didn't pay too much attention to the campaigning. She was a dyed-in-the-wool Democrat who admired President Roosevelt intensely. From her point of view, she had too much to do to worry with anything beyond getting into town on Election Day to vote for him.

Mammaw had not only me to take care of, but also Allen, a newborn. Together we constituted a terrific load for a fifty-three year old woman.

Fortunately, by the time Allen came along with all his diapers, she no longer had to wash clothes by hand. That chore was always among the worst farmwomen faced. Many days I've seen her outside in the backyard, building a fire under a black washpot. When her water was boiling, she'd stick a rubboard into a washtub of soapy water. Against its ribbed metal surface, she'd rub homemade lye soap into soiled spots on clothing, sheets, and towels. She'd toss the soapy garments into the boiling water and stir them with a stick.

When she judged them clean, she'd fish them out with the same stick and rinse them by hand with more hot water. Then she'd push them through a hand ringer and hang them on the clothesline. The next day she'd iron with flatirons heated on the stove. She lighted kerosene lamps at night.

Then just in time for Allen came FDR's Rural Electrification.

A miracle! Surely, when God said, "Let there be light," He was only a step ahead of what Roosevelt did with the passage of that one bill.

At a cost she could afford, Mammaw had electric lights put in our house. From outlets set in the center of the high ceilings, light bulbs swung on four

Then she sat on a blanket beside the car and watched us. If one of us stepped off in a hole, she was on her feet in an instant reeling us in. Allen became quite a swimmer, but I was too bony for natural buoyancy. While I liked to run up and down the beach, collect shells, and build sandcastles, I never really liked the salty water.

Of course, she watched us like a hawk to see that we didn't become over-tired. After a picnic on a quilt with a tablecloth and napkins, she'd supervise our sandcastles. She'd put her bare foot down on the sand and we'd pack sand around it. If we'd made strong walls, the castle wouldn't collapse when she pulled her foot out.

Those days at the beach were some of the most joyous of our lives.

And Mammaw wasn't through with Allen yet.

Because in Texas almost every grown man carried a rifle or a shotgun and knew how to use it, Allen must become a hunter. Hunting had the advantage of being both manly and gentlemanly. According to Mammaw, Grandpaw Bevens walked the Arkansas fields in the fall and brought in braces of ducks and a wild turkey or two.

So Mammaw bought Allen a BB gun. Thereafter, tubes of shot became his favorite inexpensive gift for Christmas and birthdays. Very soon, he shot a hole in her dresser mirror. Next, he put a hole through the kitchen window.

Several times he narrowly missed me where I sat perched on a limb in the salt cedars. He said he was shooting at a bird, but I knew he was aiming near me on purpose. I screamed and snarled and threatened to tell Mammaw. Now that he had grown a little more, he was giving as good as he got torment-ing me about as much as I tormented him.

Still, the BB's were creating a problem. Mammaw realized she had to teach him to use a gun safely. She loaded us in the car and drove to a forty-acre section of unimproved land, where he could hunt to his heart's content without breaking or damaging something. She drew tablet-paper targets and tacked them on the trunks of mesquite trees. He shot thousands of BB's at them. Soon he was knocking real sparrows and blackbirds out of the salt ce-dars. I still wasn't happy about his shooting at "my" trees, but fortunately he quickly grew tired of it.

Almost from the beginning, he realized that a gun of any kind wasn't a toy. He wanted to hunt "real" birds—quail and whitewing dove. Mammaw drove him back to a section of uncleared land and let him blast away at what-ever flew buy. He actually did bring down a few that she dutifully dressed and prepared for him to eat.

All Mammaw's hard work paid off. Allen went on to become a SCUBA diver and even guided deer hunters a few seasons. He sang and entertained on rafting trips down the Rio Grande when he wasn't singing in clubs and